FAST FACTS®
ON
ROMAN CATHOLICISM

John Ankerberg
&John Weldon

HARVEST HOUSE PUBLISHERS

EUGENE, OREGON

Cover by Terry Dugan Design, Minneapolis, Minnesota

FAST FACTS® ON ROMAN CATHOLICISM
Some material previously released in *Protestants and Catholics: Do They Now Agree?* and
The Facts on Roman Catholicism
Copyright © 2004 by John Ankerberg and John Weldon
Published by Harvest House Publishers
Eugene, Oregon 97402
www.harvesthousepublishers.com

Harvest House Publishers, Inc., is the exclusive licensee of the federally registered trademark FAST FACTS.

Library of Congress Cataloging-in-Publication Data
Ankerberg, John, 1945–
    Fast facts on Roman Catholicism / John Ankerberg and John Weldon.
        p.   cm.
    Includes bibliographical references.
        ISBN 0-7369-1077-8 (pbk.)
    1. Catholic Church. I. Weldon, John. II. Title.
        BX891.3.A55 2004
        282—dc22   2003020279

Printed in the United States of America

04   05   06   07   08   09   10   11   12   / DP-KB /   10   9   8   7   6   5   4   3   2   1

Contents

Section VIII
Catholics, Protestants, and the Bible

Section IX
Catholics and Protestants Together?

Section X
The Nature of a Christian Church

To those who love Good News

❧

"Test yourselves to make sure you
are solid in the faith."

—2 CORINTHIANS 13:5 THE MESSAGE

Understanding and Evaluating Roman Catholicism

The purpose of this book is twofold: first, to help non-Catholic Christians better understand what Roman Catholicism believes and practices; and second, to help Roman Catholics evaluate their own church on the basis of biblical teaching. The latter is necessary since, as Catholic apologist Karl Keating points out in *What Catholics Really Believe—Setting the Record Straight*, "Catholics are required to hold and believe all the declared doctrines of the Church."[1]

All sincere Christians have a desire to honor God in their lives as much as possible. It is the hope of the authors that the information in this book will be useful to Catholics and non-Catholics as a means to evaluate what is or is not biblical, as well as an encouragement to greater commitment to God and His Word.

No one can deny that substantial changes have occurred in the Roman Catholic Church since Vatican II (1962–1965), the major council intended "to usher in the beginning of a new era in Roman Catholic history."[2] Since Vatican II, the Catholic Church has, in some quarters, increasingly encouraged its members to read the Bible and apply it to their lives. Also, it is no longer a serious sin to attend non-Catholic churches. Protestantism itself has been upgraded from the condition of being in dreadful apostasy and heresy to that of merely being composed of "separated brethren." Perhaps the most important change in Rome, again at least in some quarters, is its allowance of a new freedom for the biblical gospel itself.

Modern Roman Catholicism is commendable in other areas. For example, socially, the Church has consistently opposed abortion and maintained a high view of the sanctity of life and of marriage. It has correctly opposed the homosexual activism that, if not checked, will destroy our culture. Biblically, it has continued to defend the infallibility of Scripture—at least as official doctrine. Theologically, at least at one level, it generally accepts the orthodox views of the Trinity, Christ's deity, and His atonement. Spiritually, it has a good understanding of the seriousness of sin and, apart from salvation, sin's consequences in eternal judgment.

Nevertheless, this does not mean that the Church is without problems. Perhaps the most serious problem in modern Roman Catholicism is the unwillingness to accept biblical authority alone as the final means of determining Christian doctrine and practice. For example, because the Church accepts its Tradition as a means of divine revelation, even its biblically correct teachings become hedged about with embellishments that tend to revise, neutralize, or nullify biblical truths.

Jesus Himself taught that even heartfelt religious traditions can actually become a means of leading people away from God's best purpose for their lives. On one occasion Jesus even told the devoutly religious leaders of His day, "You have let go of the commands of God and are holding on to the traditions of men" (Mark 7:8).

Regardless, no one can argue with the statement that "the Roman Church has been one of the most powerful influences in the history of all civilization."[3] Because Roman Catholicism is a major world religion having some one billion adherents and because its influence in the world is so vast, it is vital to know if its basic claims are true.

ROMAN CATHOLICISM TODAY

1

HOW INFLUENTIAL IS THE ROMAN CATHOLIC CHURCH IN THE WORLD?

The Roman Catholic Church is one of the most powerful institutions on earth. In one way or another, its beliefs hold sway over literally hundreds of millions of people around the world. For example,

- almost 90 percent of Brazil is Catholic, with more than 135 million adherents

- more than 95 percent of Mexico is Catholic, with almost 90 million adherents

- about 30 percent of the U.S. is Catholic, with more than 60 million adherents

- about 85 percent of the Philippines is Catholic, with some 60 million adherents

- about 98 percent of Italy is Catholic, with more than 56 million adherents

These five countries alone have 400 million baptized Roman Catholics. France, Spain, Poland, Colombia, and Argentina are 90 to 95 percent Catholic, comprising an additional 200 million people. The rest of the world has an additional 400 million baptized Catholics. From 1978 through 2000 the global baptized Catholic population rose by almost 40 percent and, in 2001, surpassed the mark of one billion—63 percent of the population in the Americas, 40 percent in Europe, and 3 percent in Asia.[1]

Why Catholic influence matters is because every worldview, every belief system, matters. For better or worse, what people believe has consequences personally and socially. Pascal noted correctly that between heaven and hell there is only life—one of the frailest things in the world. How does one finally and authoritatively determine that one's eternal fate has been secured in heaven...rather than in a nightmare? Answering this question will take us along many avenues of Catholic and Protestant belief, but every place we travel will bear upon this single most important issue.

2

WHAT ARE THE GROUPINGS FOUND IN ROMAN CATHOLICISM TODAY, AND WHY ARE THEY IMPORTANT FOR UNDERSTANDING CATHOLICISM?

The issues surrounding Catholic belief and authority are compounded by the fact there are some ten groupings into which Roman Catholicism around the world falls. The distinctions between them are often not clear because they tend to overlap. Nor would individual Catholics necessarily agree with the suggested labels. But they will serve for purposes of illustration:

1. *Nominal or social Catholicism*—the Roman Catholicism of the largely uncommitted—perhaps those born or married into the Church but who have little knowledge of Rome's theology. They are principally Catholics in name only, although, because of infant baptism, still Catholics allegedly "in Christ."

2. *Syncretistic–eclectic Catholicism*—the Roman Catholicism that is, to varying degrees, combined with or absorbed by the pagan religion of the indigenous culture in which it exists (for example, as in South America and Africa).

3. *Traditional or orthodox Catholicism*—the most powerful and conservative branch of Roman Catholicism which holds to papal authority and historic Church doctrines, such as those reasserted at the Council of Trent.* Among this group may be classified the ultratraditionalist Catholics who adamantly reject Vatican II and generally distrust modern changes (for example, abandoning the Latin Mass).[1] Also included are traditionalist Catholics who, while adhering to the entirety of creedal Catholicism and papal authority, more or less accept Vatican II reforms and yet staunchly reject liberalism.

4. *"Moderate" Catholicism*—the Roman Catholicism of post–Vatican II that is neither entirely traditional nor entirely liberal.

5. *Modernist, liberal Catholicism*—the post–Vatican II "progressive" Roman Catholicism that to varying degrees rejects traditional doctrine.

6. *Ethnic, or cultural, Catholicism*—often retained by migrants to America who use their religion "to provide a sense of belonging. They feel that not to be Roman Catholic is not to belong and to lose [their] nationality and roots."[2]

7. *Lapsed or apostate Catholicism*—the Roman Catholicism that involves alienated, backslidden, or apostate Catholics who are largely indifferent to the Church and its God.

---

* The Council of Trent was the major Catholic gathering (1545–1563) that reaffirmed and decreed official Catholic doctrine in response to the Protestant Reformation.

8. *Charismatic Catholicism*—the Roman Catholicism that seeks to accept the "baptism of the Holy Spirit" and speaking in tongues and other spiritual gifts as signs of a deeper Catholic spirituality. (In certain ways this illustrates the related, though often distinct, grouping of mystical Catholicism, which is undergirded by the mystical and sometimes Eastern–occult writings of Catholic mystics.)

9. *"Evangelical" Catholicism*—former Protestant evangelicals converted to Rome, who may retain some of their former beliefs but who now accept Roman Catholicism as the one true church and its doctrines as authoritative. In large measure these persons are no longer evangelicals.

10. *Evangelical "Catholicism"*—former Roman Catholics who are truly evangelical and who have rejected the unbiblical teachings of Rome, often deciding to remain in the Church to help reform it or as a means to evangelize other Catholics. In large measure these persons are no longer Catholics.

If we consider several of these groupings in a bit more detail, we will be better able to understand modern Catholicism.

The *traditionalists* are the most influential segment of the Church because through the Pope, bishops, and orthodox priests they occupy the center of power in Catholicism. Traditionalists believe that by being obedient to the Church they are, in essence, being obedient to God and Christ. Why? Because they have been taught that whatever the Church decrees as orthodox belief and practice through its tradition is, by definition, the will of God.[3] Thus, for one to obey the Church is equivalent to submitting to what God has revealed as His will for one's life. As a result, the traditional Catholic feels no need to examine the Bible for himself to determine whether or not what the Church teaches is in accord with it. This is because he or she has been taught that the Church has been granted divine power to interpret the Bible infallibly. Therefore, such a person completely trusts whatever the Church says as being biblical.

The *modernists,* or liberal branch of the Church, are "liberal" largely in relationship to the authority of Rome, not necessarily in the Protestant sense of being primarily rationalistic. Liberal Catholics vary widely in the degree to which they have departed from traditional Catholicism. One example would be that of Catholic theologians who may question the legitimacy of papal infallibility—or the Church's teaching on justification or birth control—but who otherwise seek to remain loyal to Rome. A differing example would be the Marxist-oriented "liberation theology" of many Central and South American priests and theologians, whose primary concern is more with "political liberation" and "social justice" than anything principally biblical or spiritual.

Nevertheless, although the term "liberal" is used specifically in relationship to the authority of Rome, there are also many Catholic leaders who are more or less liberal in a Protestant sense, in that they reject biblical authority, apply rationalistic higher critical methods to biblical study, deny Christ's unique deity, teach universalism, and so on.

Charismatic Catholics emphasize faith as a personal commitment to Jesus and loyalty to Scripture. This branch of Catholicism frequently encourages Bible studies, speaking in tongues, and oftentimes a "born-again" or "baptism in the Spirit" experience. But more frequently than not, it seems to still remain Roman Catholic, attempting to integrate newfound faith and experience with traditional doctrines involving Mary, papal authority, and the sacraments. Moreover, in practice the Catholic experience of the "baptism in the Holy Spirit" often leads to greater devotion to Catholic belief and practice. For example, thousands of Catholics have reported how the "baptism in the Spirit" affected them in terms like the following: "The mother of God has become more special." "I have a deeper devotion to Mary." "I have taken up the Rosary since baptism in the Spirit."[4]

Evangelical "Catholics" are truly evangelical believers and not Catholics. In other words, they are not committed Roman Catholics who merely appropriate the title of evangelical Christian. They understand the issues doctrinally and spiritually and attempt to walk what can be a very difficult (and to some people's minds, inconsistent) line of fidelity to the Bible while remaining members of the Roman Catholic Church. That this line can occasionally be successfully negotiated is known personally to coauthor Weldon. A friend of his in Bible school had such a love for Catholics that he found a parish that not only accepted his evangelical training as priestly ordination but whose superiors permitted him to teach the Bible in its entirety on the basis of personal conscience (that is, as an evangelical Protestant). Not that it was easy: His parish got so much Bible that many of them decided they were no longer Catholics, while others attempted a synthesis of evangelicalism and Catholicism. (How the situation finally ended, we were unable to determine.)

3

Why Is a Book on Catholicism Relevant to Protestants and Vice Versa?

This book is relevant because it concentrates on the issue of truth, something both groups claim to honor. But truth is not necessarily easy to find. In recent years, there has been a significant increase of lay Catholic apologetic works, and this has caused many mainline and even some evangelical Protestants to leave their faith and join with Rome. So on that point alone, this topic clearly has relevance for Protestants. Catholic apologists and evangelical converts to Rome such as Dr. Scott Hahn, Karl

Keating, Mark Shea, David Currie, and Stephen Ray have lectured widely and written books on the issue.*

These authors seem to have found a critical weakness among many evangelicals—adequately defending *sola scriptura,* the Scripture's authority over the church—which leaves some evangelicals who cannot defend their faith open to conversion. [1]

On the other hand, even Catholics acknowledge that millions worldwide have left Rome and joined evangelical or fundamental Protestantism. Indeed, there are also millions of people with one foot in each camp, attempting what is at best a difficult balancing act.

Committed Catholics and Protestants are each convinced their faith is *both* Christian and biblical, accurately following the teachings of Jesus and the apostles. However, each group disagrees as to the legitimacy of the other's claim. Here is the good news: While both might be wrong, only one can be right.

The purpose of life is knowing God personally—in the end, nothing else matters. But how does one know God personally? If you can't wait for the answer, read the conclusion. In the meantime, the remainder of this book will take a journey through these two great faiths and document why we believe our conclusions about their claims are true.

---

* *Rome Sweet Home: Our Journey to Catholicism* (Hahn); *The Usual Suspects: Answering Anti-Catholic Fundamentalists* (Keating); *By What Authority?: An Evangelical Discovers Catholic Tradition* (Shea); *Born Fundamentalist, Born Again Catholic* (Currie); and *Crossing the Tiber: Evangelical Protestants Discover the Historical Church* (Ray).

SECTION II

THE CRITICAL ISSUE OF DIVINE AUTHORITY

4

IS THE BIBLE ALONE THE FINAL AUTHORITY, OR IS IT THE CHURCH?

You must teach what is in accord with sound doctrine.
—the apostle Paul's instructions to Titus in Titus 2:1

Because of what is at stake—and here both Protestants and Catholics agree it is the difference between heaven and hell—neither group can escape the obligation to be certain that their own convictions are true, and independently verified as such. No one should risk everything by taking someone else's word that salvation means this but not that. This takes us to the heart of the matter, which involves the issue of divine authority. Who has the authority to tell us that salvation is either this or that? Is final authority found in the Bible, or is it found in the Church? In sum, Protestants believe that the Bible alone is the supreme authority for deciding matters of faith (doctrine) and practice. Catholics believe the Roman Catholic Church holds that authority. If Roman Catholicism is correct, Protestants are in serious trouble because they have undermined, divided, and distorted Christ's true church. If Protestantism is correct, Roman Catholics are in that boat because they have undermined and distorted the teachings of Scripture, which point out the true way to salvation.

Protestants and Catholics disagree on specific doctrines not because the matters that divide them are irresolvable, but largely because of a few contrary premises that are held. These premises are simple to examine in the light of Scripture and history. Once the correct premises are determined, very logical consequences follow. Whether you are Catholic or Protestant, you owe it to your own interests to examine these arguments. In other words, the few hours you spend with this book could be the most important of your life.

The Issue of Divine Authority

What constitutes divine revelation is crucial because, without it, very little can be known about God—who He is, what He has communicated to us, and what He expects of us. The question of divine authority is indivisibly bound to the issue of divine revelation. Only that which comes from God has divine authority. Only God's revelation has authentic and inherent power to command obedience.

Has God spoken? If so, where has He spoken? Protestants have traditionally maintained that God has spoken solely in the 39 books of the Old Testament and the 27 books of the New Testament. Only these books are divinely authoritative because only these are inspired by God Himself. Protestants believe the Bible can be individually understood and applied to one's life without the need for an official church interpreter. In a word, for Protestants, the *Bible* is the only divine authority.

For Catholics, in sum, the *Church* is the final authority, not the Bible. The Church determines what and who has divine authority and how to interpret divine revelation. Roman Catholicism teaches that, in addition to the Protestant Bible, there are five other sources having divine authority, each source's credibility being guaranteed by the Church.

1. There are *additional books* written between the Old and New Testaments, known to Catholics as the *deutero-canonical books* and to Protestants as the *Apocrypha*. As of 1546, Roman Catholics consider these books genuine Scripture and include them as part of their Bible.

2. Catholicism maintains that divine authority is to be found in the *authorized tradition* of the Roman Catholic Church, which is also classified as the "Word of God."[1] For example, when the Pope adds to *canon law*—the law governing the Church—he is in effect writing new Scripture by adding divine revelation (new tradition) upon divine revelation (existing tradition).[2]

3. As of the council known as Vatican I (1869–1870), full divine authority (infallibility) is given to the *papal office* when the Pope speaks *ex cathedra* ("from the chair")—that is, officially on matters of faith and morals as the teacher of the church. (See question 32 for more information.)

4. When speaking or teaching in conjunction with the Pope and orthodox Catholic tradition, Roman Catholic *bishops* are also held to be infallible, and hence divinely authoritative.

5. The *official interpretation of the Bible* (Roman Catholic teaching) is considered to have divine warrant and authority.

In essence, all five of these sources can be summarized under the term *Roman Catholic Tradition*.

The Achilles' heel of Roman Catholicism is this very concept of tradition, which ultimately exerts final authority over Scripture. Many Church teachings may be authoritative Catholic doctrine, but they cannot be found in the Bible. As Jesus told the Pharisees and teachers of the law, "Isaiah was right when he prophesied about you....You have let go of the commands of God and are holding on to the traditions of men....Thus you nullify the word of God by your tradition that you have handed down" (Mark 7:6,8,13).

Authority by Definition

In the end, whatever Rome's *magisterium,* the teaching office of the Church, says is true, is true by definition. The teaching alone is proof of its validity, irrespective of Scripture. For example, Catholic apologist Karl Keating says of the alleged bodily assumption of Mary into heaven—which is nowhere stated or implied in the Bible—"The mere fact that the church teaches the doctrine of the assumption as definitely true is a guarantee that it is true."[3]

It seems that one ends up with a church that can teach whatever it pleases with no scriptural or other safeguard as to the truth of the teaching. The truth is "whatever we say it is"—and that ends the matter.

The key difference between the Roman Catholic and Protestant approach to divine authority is illustrated in the following statement by Catholic book reviewer John Knox. Knox explains why the book *The Gospel According to Rome,* by former Catholic priest James G. McCarthy, is incorrect despite its thoroughly biblical emphasis. It is because only the Catholic Church can properly interpret the Bible, not an individual person. McCarthy was doomed from the start because he sought to interpret the Bible by himself, apart from the teachings of Rome:

> To understand the Bible properly, it must be read through the eyeglasses of the Church, since it is the Church whose mission it is to guard, guarantee, and interpret the Sacred pages....The Bible is not the only source of faith, as Luther taught in the sixteenth century, for without the intervention of a divine, infallible teaching apostolate distinct from the Bible, we could never know with divine certainty what books constitute the inspired Scriptures, nor what the Sacred books mean. The Bible itself is but a dead letter calling for a divine interpreter....Christ never said that the

Bible would contain all His divine revelation....The mere appeal to the Bible or to history is therefore beside the point.[4]

To the contrary, it all depends on what constitutes divine authority. If persuasive evidence requires the conclusion that the Bible alone constitutes divine revelation, and equally persuasive evidence disqualifies Catholic Tradition as having divine authority, the "mere appeal to the Bible" is established as the only game in town. Thus, Protestantism rejects the additional sources of divine authority in Catholicism. It underscores this as the single most important division between the two churches, the one division that leads to all others, the one fatal premise.

Divine authority cannot be found in the Bible alone and at the same time in various additional sources of alleged revelation when these deny biblical teaching. Because God does not contradict Himself (2 Corinthians 1:17-20; see also Psalm 145:13; Galatians 3:21; Hebrews 13:8) and cannot lie (Titus 1:2), He cannot affirm one set of teachings in the Bible and then declare them wrong through additional forms of revealed Tradition. Therefore, Protestants believe that if the Bible truly is God's Word (as Catholics also maintain), then anything that conflicts with biblical teaching cannot possibly originate from God or be accepted as having divine authority, no matter what its source.

5

WHY DO PROTESTANTS BELIEVE THAT THE BIBLE ALONE IS AUTHORITATIVE AND INERRANT (FREE FROM ERROR)?

As we will see, the Bible asserts or assumes its inerrancy throughout its pages. But it is important to realize that inerrancy is inseparably bound, not only to the doctrine of revelation, but also to the nature of God Himself. Why?

First, God's revelation of Himself occurred through a very specific manner—*verbal, plenary inspiration.* (*Plenary* means absolute and unqualified.) This means that the divine inspiration of the Bible involves its very words (Matthew 4:4; Romans 3:2) and extends equally to every part of Scripture. This is why the Bible declares that "all Scripture is inspired by God" (2 Timothy 3:16 NASB).

Second, the Bible reveals that God is a God of truth and that His nature is holy and righteous; therefore, He is incapable of lying. If divine inspiration extends to every word of the Bible, the entire Bible must be considered free of error. In other words, if God is incapable of inspiring error, whatever He inspires is inerrant.

Finally, the Bible also reveals that God is omnipotent, or all-powerful. This means He was able to safeguard the process of inspiration from error even though the Bible was given through fallible men. In light of this, it must be concluded that whatever God speaks is inerrant, and since every word of the Bible is God's Word, therefore the entire Bible is without error.

In order to establish the Bible alone as the only source of divine authority, we need to prove that, first, the Bible claims to be the inerrant Word of God, and second, that these claims are justified. If these are the case, then anything that contradicts what the Bible teaches cannot, logically, have divine authority, whether in Catholic or Protestant tradition.

The Old Testament

The Old Testament is either God's Word or a fraud because it repeatedly asserts its divine authority (for example, Isaiah 40:8). The phrase "Thus says the Lord" or a similar expression is used within it some 2,800 times (Jeremiah 1:2; see also Exodus 34:27; Deuteronomy 18:18; 1 Kings 22:14; Isaiah 8:19-20; Jeremiah 36:29; Amos 3). Inspiration (involving inerrancy) is explicitly asserted for almost 70 percent of the Old Testament, or 26 of its 39 books.[1] The remainder has its divine authority confirmed through other means, such as predictive prophecy and scientific prevision that cannot be explained in any other way (see 2 Peter 1:20-21), and also by the authority of Christ.

New Testament assertions about the verbal, plenary inspiration of the Old Testament provide additional corroboration. We find that more than 90 percent of the Old Testament books have their authority, authenticity, or both directly affirmed by the New Testament.[2] For example, in the book of Hebrews, the phrase "God said" or its equivalent occurs many times just prior to quotations from specific books of the Old Testament, such as Psalms (Hebrews 1:6-12; 4:7), Jeremiah (8:8-12; 10:15-17), Haggai (12:26), Deuteronomy (13:5), and others.

Especially relevant are the pronouncements of Jesus, who, as God incarnate (in human form), speaks infallibly (see Matthew 24:35; John 5:46; 7:16; 8:14-16,26,28; 12:48-50; 14:6; and compare Philippians 2; Titus 2:13; 2 Peter 1:20-21; John 1:14). In John 17:17, Jesus said, "Your word is truth" and in Matthew 4:4, "Man shall not live on bread alone, but on every word that proceeds out of the mouth of God" (NASB). In both instances He could have referred only to the Jewish Scriptures—our Protestant Old Testament (see Luke 24:27). Jesus, who *is* God, affirmed 100 percent of the Old Testament as inspired and inerrant.[3]

The New Testament

Jesus indicated more than once that new revelation from God was forthcoming. For example, He promised the disciples that the Holy Spirit would teach them all things and bring to their remembrance the things they were taught by Him (John 14:26), referring at least in part to the Gospels (see Matthew 24:35). He also promised that the Holy Spirit would guide them into all the truth (John 16:12-15), which includes the remainder of the New Testament. Thus, it is not surprising that "virtually every New Testament writer claimed that his writing was divinely authoritative....The cumulative effect of this self-testimony is an overwhelming confirmation that the New Testament writers claimed inspiration."[4]

Indeed, the New Testament writers assumed their writing was as binding as the Old Testament (for example, see 1 Timothy 5:18; 2 Peter 3:15-16). This asserts a great deal. These writers were orthodox Jews who believed God's Word had theretofore been confined to the known Old Testament *canon*—the authoritative books accepted as Holy Scripture. To add to this body of holy writings was a terrible presumption unless new revelation were truly being given.

But the writers' recognition of new revelation did not come unprepared. The very fact of the arrival of the long-prophesied Messiah and the New Covenant (as mentioned by Isaiah, Jeremiah, Ezekiel, and others), coupled with the incarnation and atonement of God Himself (John 1:14; Philippians 2:1-9), all but demanded a corresponding body of divinely inspired literature to explain and expound these events (see Galatians 3:8; and again, John 16:12-15). God had no more likely candidates for the giving of this revelation than the apostles of His own Son, or those they approved. And perhaps for even more credibility, the former skeptic and persecutor of the church, the great apostle Paul, was commissioned by God to write a full one-fourth of the entire new revelation, while the exacting physician and historian Luke wrote another one-fourth.

How could Jesus, the incarnate God, teach the inerrancy of the divinely inspired Old Testament and not know that the same condition would apply to the divinely inspired New Testament? Is it credible to believe that Jesus thought the Holy Spirit, the "Spirit of Truth," who inspired the New Testament (see John 16:13-15), would corrupt His own words or inspire error? Perhaps one reason Jesus never wrote anything was because He knew it was unnecessary: The Holy Spirit would inspire an inerrant Word. How else could He teach (or could we reasonably believe), "My words will never pass away" (Matthew 24:35)?

"Untainted by Any Error"

Regardless, is it proper to call errant writings "holy"? How would inspiration be divine if it allowed for the presence of truth *and* error? Would not the Bible simply be human and like every other book—and deserve to be treated like every other book? If we answer "no" by appealing to its unique theological content, how do we really know such content is true?

If God's Word is eternal, how can it be flawed? What did God mean when He called His Word "tested," "holy," "perfect," "pure" "righteous," "good," "trustworthy," and "true"—for example, "All your words are true; all your righteous laws are eternal" (Psalm 119:160)?[5] On this issue of inerrancy, the great expositor Charles Spurgeon once spoke of the implications:

> This is the book untainted by any error, but is pure, unalloyed, perfect truth. Why? Because God wrote it. Ah! charge God with error if you please; tell Him that His book is not what it ought to be.[6]

6

HOW DO WE KNOW THAT CLAIMS FOR THE DIVINE INSPIRATION AND INERRANCY OF THE BIBLE ARE JUSTIFIED?

There are numerous converging lines of evidence that, for all practical purposes, prove the Bible really is God's only revelation to mankind. For example, scores of detailed predictions of the future that were later fulfilled literally are found only in the Bible—and can only be explained on the basis of divine inspiration. No one can accurately predict the future in detail unless they already know it, and only God possesses such a capacity (see 2 Peter 1:21-22).[1]

However, the area we wish to stress here is simply the authority of Jesus Christ Himself. It is a historical fact that Jesus is the only person who conquered death by permanently rising from the dead, something He predicted on at least a dozen occasions. He is the only person who makes it possible, through His atoning sacrifice, for His followers to enter God's kingdom. His unparalleled teachings and miracles, added to His resurrection, prove the truth of His many claims to be God in human form. If so, then He is an infallible authority. And in that role He declared the Old Testament to be the inspired Word of God, pre-authenticated the New Testament (Matthew 24:35; John 14:26), and personally inspired its final book (Revelation 1:1-3).

Did Jesus ever express any doubts about Scripture? Did He warn His church that the New Testament revelation would be incomplete or corrupted? Indeed, the strength of the case for inerrancy can only be seen by a detailed study of Jesus' absolute trust in and use of Scripture.[2] For Jesus, what Scripture said, God said—period. Not once did He say, "This Scripture is incorrect," and proceed to amend it. If Jesus was God, then He was correct in His view of Scripture: The Bible truly is the literally revealed, inerrant Word of God, and only it has final authority. Perhaps more relevant to our topic, Jesus never accepted Jewish tradition as a final authority; to the contrary, He warned His followers that it had seriously corrupted God's revelation (for example, Matthew 15:6).

If God cannot lie, never changes, and can be trusted to never contradict Himself, then only one conclusion follows: Whatever or whoever denies what God has revealed in the Bible cannot logically claim divine authority. Nowhere in the Bible does God tell us to accept anything that contradicts what He has said is true in His Word. To give our allegiance to church traditions that are contrary to Scripture, from whatever source or church, or to people who claim divine authority but deny Biblical teaching, is to take away the rightful place God alone should occupy in our lives.

A Well-Tested Claim

As to inerrancy properly defined,[3] not only does the Bible teach it, but the facts of history, archaeology, textual criticism, and science prove it true.[4] If critics could irrefutably demonstrate an error in Scripture, they would have done so in the last 2,000 years, but they never have. This isn't merely our claim, it's been tested.

For example, Gleason L. Archer was an undergraduate classics major who received training in Latin, Greek, French, and German at Harvard University. At seminary he majored in Hebrew, Aramaic, and Arabic, and in postgraduate study became involved with the ancient languages of Akkadian and Syriac, teaching courses on these subjects. He has had a special interest in Middle-Kingdom Egyptian studies (Egypt from about 2040–1640 B.C.) and at the Oriental Institute in Chicago did specialized study in Eighteenth Dynasty (Egypt from about 1550–1295 B.C.) historical records, as well as studying Coptic and Sumerian.

Dr. Archer has also spent extensive time in the Holy Land, where he has visited most of the important biblical archaeological sites, and he worked in Beirut, Lebanon, on a specialized study of modern literary Arabic. He holds one degree from Princeton Theological Seminary and a PhD from Harvard Graduate School. Further, he has done extensive studies in archaeology and other areas relative to the biblical text, become fluent in 15 languages, and received full training in the law and legal evidences. This background has enabled him to become expert in the issue of alleged errors or contradictions in Scripture. Here is his conclusion about alleged errors in the extant copies of Scripture:

> In my opinion this charge can be refuted and its falsity exposed by an objective study done in a consistent, evangelical perspective....I candidly believe I have been confronted with just about all the biblical difficulties under discussion in theological circles today—especially those pertaining to the interpretation and defense of Scripture....As I have dealt with one apparent discrepancy after another and have studied the alleged contradictions

between the biblical record and the evidence of linguistics, archaeology, or science, my confidence in the trustworthiness of Scripture has been repeatedly verified and strengthened by the discovery that almost every problem in Scripture that has ever been discovered by man, from ancient times until now, has been dealt with in a completely satisfactory manner by the biblical text itself—or else by objective archaeological information.[5]

But there are many similar testimonies from other leading scholars. Dr. Robert Dick Wilson (1856–1930), an Old Testament authority and author of *A Scientific Investigation of the Old Testament,* could read the New Testament in nine different languages by the age of 25. In addition, he could repeat from memory a Hebrew translation of the entire New Testament without missing a single syllable, and do the same with large portions of the Old Testament. He proceeded to learn 45 languages and dialects and was also a master of paleography and philology. He wrote, "I have made it an invariable habit never to accept an objection to a statement of the Old Testament without subjecting it to a most thorough investigation, linguistically and factually," and, "I defy any man to make an attack upon the Old Testament on the grounds of evidence that I cannot investigate." His conclusion? That no critic had succeeded in proving an error in the Old Testament.[6]

Theologian, philosopher, and trial attorney John Warwick Montgomery, who holds nine graduate degrees in different fields, observes, "I myself have never encountered an alleged contradiction in the Bible which could not be cleared up by the use of the original languages of the Scriptures and/or by the use of accepted principles of literary and historical interpretation." [7]

Harold O.J. Brown earned four degrees from Harvard University and Harvard Divinity School (Germanic languages and biochemical sciences, theology, church history, and a PhD in Reformation studies) and studied at the University of Marburg, Germany, and the University of Vienna, Austria. He concludes,

If it were possible to point to undeniable, substantial errors in the present Hebrew and Greek texts of Scripture, it would certainly suggest the presumption that the originals had errors. The fact that it is still possible today to claim the autographs (orginal manuscripts) were inerrant is an indication that no one has yet succeeded in showing there is even one substantial, undeniable error or contradiction in our present copies.[8]

And noted theologian J.I. Packer comes to this conclusion: "No compelling necessity springs from modern knowledge to conclude that Scripture errs anywhere."[9]

The conclusion is that the miraculous nature of the Bible itself—which speaks for its inspiration and hence inerrancy—the infallible pronouncements of God incarnate on an inerrant Scripture, and the data of the text itself are sufficient reasons to accept the proposition that the Bible is inerrant. Only the Bible has the authority to command our obedience because only the Bible has divine authority.

THE MOST IMPORTANT ISSUE: FINDING THE WAY TO HEAVEN

7

WHY ARE THE BIBLICAL DOCTRINES OF SALVATION AND JUSTIFICATION SO REMARKABLE?

These doctrines are so amazing that words fail to adequately nourish the implications. Despite the existence of literally thousands of religions, large and small, these teachings are never found outside biblical religion. They are remarkable in that the most unthinkable thing in the universe actually happens—something we will now explore.

The Bad News

We have offended a holy God far more than we can imagine. Indeed, our perception of our offenses is infinitely incomplete, as it were. God exists in eternity in absolute perfection, infinite in holiness, justice, and righteousness. His power and knowledge have no limits. According to the Bible, God is so holy and hates sin so thoroughly that His eternal infinite wrath remains directed against it. Only His love and mercy guard the floodgates of punishment. Those who have read Jonathan Edwards' "Sinners in the Hands of an Angry God,"[1] one of the more famous and powerful sermons of the eighteenth century, have some small idea of the perils faced by the unforgiven. (See excerpt in note 1 to this question.)

This God is so powerful that He can instantaneously speak into existence a universe of trillions and trillions of suns from nothing. To give one an idea of what we are talking about, a million earths will fit into our sun, but a million of our suns will fit into endless other suns in the universe. We can be badly burned on the beach by the fires of just one little star about 100 million miles away. That little star—our sun—burns at a 10,000-degree surface temperature and a 27-million-degree core temperature, yet its fierce heat is like ice compared to other stars. In our galaxy 100 billion known stars; in the universe we "know" of, 100 billion galaxies— a total of 10 sextillion stars (10,000,000,000,000,000,000,000)— spoken into existence from nothing. And that's only a microscopic display of omnipotence.

But God's holiness is also infinite. If our comprehension of God's power is minuscule, so is our understanding of His holiness. That's one reason the Bible warns people to "flee from the wrath to come." Outside of Christ, no one will stand before the throne of His infinite justice. That's the bad news.

The Good News

But the good news is very good. This awesome and fearful God is so astonishingly loving He actually *became* a man—an act much more humbling than, for example, our becoming an insect. He became a man not merely to attempt communication. He became a man to *die for us*. To die for human sin—subject to His own full divine wrath against sin, in His own Person, on the cross.

If you had the power, would you become an insect, let alone die for an insect, let alone be tortured on a cross for an insect's welfare?

> Very rarely will anyone die for a righteous man, though for
> a good man someone might possibly dare to die. But God

demonstrates his own love for us in this: While we were still sinners, Christ died for us (Romans 5:7-8).

This is what separates Christianity from every other religion in the world—and in G.K. Chesterton's words, makes "dust and nonsense" out of comparative religion. Only Christianity has good news for the world; other religions have no news at all.

The biblical doctrine of justification presents the unique teaching that, in *fact,* any man or woman on earth may be fully forgiven *all* his or her sins, past, present, and future, regardless of severity, and declared absolutely, utterly, perfectly, and eternally righteous before God—simply on the basis of trust in Christ. Not the smallest portion of a single good work, or the smallest aspect of personal merit or righteousness, is required to forgive one's sins—*only* genuine faith in Christ.

Luther was certainly correct when he wrote that, in the end, there were only two religions in the world: the religion of works and the religion of grace. It should get a person thinking that, among the thousands of religions in the world, there is only one that teaches salvation by grace through faith alone: biblical Christianity. How did such a religion ever originate if not by divine revelation? (Luther was also correct that, while faith alone saves, the faith that saves is not alone—but more on that in question 10.)

The Problem of Grace

The joyous news of this doctrine is precisely what makes it so controversial. People have a natural tendency to want to earn their own way to heaven because they want some part of the glory. They resist the idea of free grace—which of course wasn't free to God at all: His only Son was tortured and died on the cross to provide forgiveness. To be sure, there are other religions that use the terms "grace" or "salvation by faith," but they mean something entirely different than what the Bible teaches. Always involved is some form of cooperation with God, so that He accomplishes part of salvation and we accomplish the rest. By this thinking, in eternity, we are legitimately capable of boasting about our salvation, for our salvation truly depended, in part, upon us. But the Bible declares that, because salvation is 100 percent by grace, this is not possible: "Where, then, is boasting? It is excluded" (Romans 3:27).

Knowing whether salvation is by works or by grace is the most important issue for any person anywhere. The reason is simple: Justification and the difference it makes is the difference between heaven and hell. If, as the Bible teaches, the only way to heaven is by grace alone through faith in Christ alone, but we add required works of merit, then we may not make it to heaven at all. Why? Because we are ultimately not trusting fully and entirely upon Christ's sacrifice on our behalf, but upon ourselves.

However, because we are imperfect, confronting a standard impossible for us to meet, we don't have the ability to merit even one sliver of our salvation. The apostle Paul understood this perfectly, which is why he was so inflexible with those who attempted to insert works into the gospel of grace:

> I am astonished that you are so quickly deserting the one who called you by the grace of Christ and are turning to a different gospel—which is really no gospel at all. Evidently some people are throwing you into confusion and are trying to pervert the gospel of Christ. But even if we or an angel from heaven should preach a gospel other than the one we preached to you, let him be eternally condemned! As we have already said, so now I say again: If anybody is preaching to you a gospel other than what you accepted, let him be eternally condemned!" (Galatians 1:6-9).

That's why he also wrote to his critics,

> I am not ashamed of the gospel, because it is the *power of God* for the salvation of everyone who believes" (Romans 1:16).

God declares there is only one way of salvation: by believing in His Son. This is the true gospel (see John 3:16; 6:47; Romans 11:6; Galatians 2–3; 1 John 5:13). If works are added, there is no gospel at all—rather, to quote a scripture from a different context, "only a fearful expectation of judgment" (Hebrews 10:27). Put simply, the gospel is not something to trifle with when eternal consequences are at stake.

Nevertheless, most Catholics and even many Protestants seek to incorporate good works in various ways, whether through the sacraments, through *legalism* (according to Webster, "strict, literal, or excessive conformity to...a religious or moral code"), or through some other means.

So how do we know beyond all doubt that personal salvation is by grace alone through faith in Christ alone, and not by individual merit or good works of any kind? Let's examine this in our next question.

8

WHAT IS THE BIBLICAL PROOF FOR THE DOCTRINE OF JUSTIFICATION BY FAITH ALONE?

If any man stands before God,
he'd better have a good lawyer.
—Peter Marshall

In one of the episodes of the popular *Star Trek: The Next Generation* TV show, an omnipotent and omniscient being named "Q"—an entity who is enigmatic, endearing, and infuriating all at once—places the entire human race on trial for its endless and sundry crimes. Captain Jean-Luc Picard does his best to justify humanity and rationalize its behavior. Not surprisingly, given the track record, "Q" isn't impressed, and the trial proceeds.

If ever the entire human race were placed on trial by a morally perfect omnipotent and omniscient being, what do you think the outcome would be? Would humanity be acquitted? On a more practical level, how would you and I fare individually before the searching gaze of infinite righteousness?

As unimaginable as it may seem to the average person, the Bible emphatically declares that this scene of divine judgment will one day be played out. In fact, Jesus Himself declared He would be the eternal Judge on the last day (Matthew 25:31-46; John 5:28-29; Revelation 20:11-15).

No doctrine is more important nor, unfortunately, more misunderstood and neglected than justification by faith alone. One thing is certain—if our salvation is dependent on our own moral perfection, no one will survive that day. Think what it would be like to stand before God and give an account for everything one ever did: every thought, every word, every deed. What excuse would one give to a holy God? If God requires a perfect record in order to enter heaven—and He does—what possible hope would anyone have? None at all.

Happily, the Bible teaches that any person who simply and truly believes in Jesus Christ as his or her personal Savior from sin is at that moment irrevocably and eternally justified. Justification is "the final verdict of God brought into the present." He not only forgives and pardons the sins of believers, but also declares them perfectly righteous by imputing (crediting) the obedience and righteousness of Christ Himself to them. It is on this basis—that of Christ's perfectly righteous life and atoning death for sin—that God "pronounces believers to have fulfilled all the requirements of the law which pertain to them."[1] Consider an illustration: If a wealthy uncle deposits a million dollars into the checking account of his young nephew, that money is now the property of his nephew—even though the boy never earned it, worked for it, or even deserved it. In justification, God "deposits" the righteousness of Jesus Christ to the believer's account—He credits the believer with the moral perfection of His own Son.

Because justification is an eternal verdict pronounced by God, it is made final the moment a person believes on Christ. "It is God who justifies. Who is he that condemns?" (Romans 8:33-34). As a result, justification is not a lifelong process like personal sanctification (individual growth in moral living), which is taught by

Catholicism. The Catholic view is that justification is a lifelong process, maintained by God and man and subject to loss by mortal sin, which is easily committed. The Protestant view is that justification is an instantaneous declaration of God unrelated to good works, personal righteousness, and individual sanctification:

Biblical	Catholic
Eternal and instant verdict	Lifelong process
Can never be lost	Can be lost
By faith alone	By personal merit

Biblical Proof

Both the Old and New Testaments teach *legal (forensic)* justification. Consider the following evidence:

> Concerning the Old Testament word *hitsdiq,* usually rendered "justified," more often than not it is "…used in a forensic or legal sense, as meaning, not 'to make just or righteous,' but 'to declare judicially that one is in harmony with the law.'"…In the Old Testament, the concept of righteousness frequently appears in a forensic or juridical context. A righteous man is one who has been declared by a judge to be free from guilt.[2]

In his book *Justification,* dissident Catholic theologian Hans Küng argues for this view when he says, "According to the original biblical usage of the term, 'justification' must be defined as a declaring just by court order."[3] Even some other Catholic theologians have agreed with Küng.[4]

The New Testament Scriptures agree with the Old, clearly showing that justification is 1) a crediting of righteousness on the basis of a person's faith, 2) a completed act of God, and 3) something that occurs wholly apart from personal merit or good works:

1. "To the man who…trusts God who justifies the wicked, *his faith is credited* as righteousness…. [How blessed is]

the man to whom God *credits righteousness* apart from works" (Romans 4:5,6).

2. "*Having been* justified by faith, we have peace with God through our Lord Jesus Christ" (Romans 5:1 NASB).

3. "We maintain that a man is justified by faith *apart from works of the Law*" (Romans 3:28 NASB).

(Please also read Luke 18:1-14; Acts 13:38-39; 15:10-11; Galatians 2:16.)

The weight of these and many other Scriptures is formidable; it is, indeed, logically impossible to deny the biblical teaching of justification by faith alone. For Roman Catholicism to say that the Bible teaches that sinners "are justified by Christ and by good works"[5] is wrong, "for in the gospel a righteousness from God is revealed, a righteousness that is *by faith* from first to last" (Romans 1:17).

Scripture clearly rules out all forms of salvation by works. And if Scripture is equally clear that salvation comes by grace through faith, then salvation must be by faith alone. To make salvation an achievement of "faith plus works" is to destroy Christ's gospel and denigrate the inestimable price paid by Christ so that salvation could be offered solely as His free gift. Please read the following Scriptures slowly and carefully:

No one will be declared righteous in his sight by observing the law; rather, through the law we become conscious of sin (Romans 3:20).

Now a righteousness from God, *apart from law,* has been made known, to which the Law and the Prophets testify (Romans 3:21).

This righteousness from God comes *through faith* in Jesus Christ to all who believe....[They] are justified *freely* [God's legal verdict pronouncing one pardoned forever] by his grace through the redemption that came by Christ Jesus (Romans 3:22,24).

God presented him [Jesus] as a sacrifice of atonement, through faith in his blood. He did this to *demonstrate his justice*...at the present time, so as to *be just and the one who justifies* those who have faith in Jesus (Romans 3:25,26).

He saved us, *not* because of righteous things we had done, but because of his mercy (Titus 3:5).

If [they are chosen] by grace, then it is *no longer by works;* if it were, grace would *no longer be grace* (Romans 11:6).

Blessed is the man whose sin the Lord will *never* count against him (Romans 4:8).

These verses teach that justification is an eternal final verdict by God—not a lifelong process—and that a person is justified by *faith alone.* There is no hint of any additional requirement, or merit, or actions (see also Romans 8:30; 10:3-4; 1 Corinthians 6:11; Galatians 3:8-13,21-25).

9

What Is the Dictionary Definition of *Justification?*

Catholic theologians maintain that Paul's use of the Greek word for *justification (dikaioō)* does *not* refer to imputed, or legally declared, righteousness. But this understanding did not come from standard Greek dictionaries. All those define the principal New Testament word for justification in a Protestant and not a Catholic sense—that is, as a legal declaration of righteousness, not an infusing of actual righteousness based upon individual merit.

As the premier Greek lexicon (Kittel's *Theological Dictionary of the New Testament*) puts it, "In Paul, the legal usage is plain and

indisputable....[It] does not suggest the infusion of moral quali-
ties [but] the justification of the ungodly who believe...the result
of a judicial pronouncement."[1] This is why Bruce Metzger, perhaps the foremost Greek scholar in America, emphasizes,

> The fact is that Paul simply does not use this verb to mean
> "to be made upright or righteous." Indeed, it is extremely
> doubtful whether it ever bore this meaning in the Greek of
> any period or author. It means "to be pronounced, or
> declared, or treated as righteous or upright."[2]

Again, standard Greek dictionaries define the Greek word for
justification as granting an imputed, not actual, righteousness.[3]
For example:

- *The Hebrew–Greek Key Word Study Bible:* "to render just
  or innocent"

- *Arndt and Gingrich:* "being acquitted, be pronounced and
  treated as righteous"

- *The New Thayer's Greek–English Lexicon:* "...which never
  means *to make* worthy, but to judge worthy, to declare
  worthy, to declare guiltless, to judge, declare, pronounce
  righteous and therefore acceptable"

- Loruv and Nida's *Greek–English Lexicon:* "the act of
  clearing someone of transgression—'to acquit, to set free,
  to remove guilt, acquittal' "

- W.E. Vine, *Expository Dictionary of New Testament
  Words:* "*dikaioō*—to declare to be righteous, to pronounce
  righteous, being the legal and formal acquittal from guilt
  by God as Judge, the pronouncement of the sinner as
  righteous, who believes on the Lord Jesus Christ"

Because of the lexical evidence, if the believer actually possesses the righteousness of Christ by divine decree, it can hardly
be called a "legal fiction," as Catholics maintain.

Catholics argue that for God to declare a sinful person righteous is inconsistent with His justice. But God says just the opposite. Because of Christ's willing substitutionary death on the cross, God is able to impute (credit) Christ's righteous status to the sinner's account and, in turn, impute the sinner's sin to Christ's account, thereby proving God *is* just:

> He did it to *demonstrate His justice* at the present time, *so as to be just* and *the one who justifies* those who have faith in Jesus" (Romans 3:26).

10

DOES THE APOSTLE JAMES CONTRADICT THE APOSTLE PAUL?

Roman Catholic scholars have difficulty dealing with passages clearly declaring justification by faith alone, such as Romans 3:21-31, because, among other reasons, they hold to the Church tradition of *self-justification*. This tradition reinterprets Scripture (similarly to tradition in some legalistically oriented Protestant churches). For example, Catholic theologians argue that their view of justification is supported in James 2:24—which, when the verse is taken out of context, seems to be true: "You see that a person is justified by what he does and not by faith alone."

James, however, is actually opposing Roman Catholic belief, not upholding it. The apostle Paul declares that true faith *alone* justifies, but that it also naturally leads to a changed life and good works. James declares that mere intellectual assent is not true faith. Thus the "faith alone" that has no works is *not* true faith—and it cannot save anyone.

James is emphasizing the fruit of a true and living faith and contrasting this with a hypocritical, dead, or intellectual "faith"—a false faith. This is clear from the context (2:14-20,26). Thus, a man may claim to have faith (verse 14), but if it's not true faith, how can it save anyone (verse 17)? Even the demons believe intellectually (verse 19), but their actions prove their hatred of God, not their faith in Him. Because true regenerating faith by definition makes a person spiritually alive to God (2 Corinthians 5:17), it will naturally lead to good works (Ephesians 2:8-10). Thus, just as a body without a spirit must be dead, so a faith without works must be dead (James 2:26). James cannot be teaching that a person is justified by law-keeping (verse 24), because he emphasizes that the least transgression of the law is what nullifies *all* law-keeping as a means of salvation (2:10; 3:2).

James does not declare that the person he speaks of has actual faith, only that he claims to: "What good is it, my brothers, if a man *claims* to have faith but has no deeds? Can such faith save him?" (2:14). Obviously, his point is that a dead or lifeless faith has no power to save. He emphasizes this again a few verses later: "Faith without deeds is useless" (verse 20). People who claim to have faith but live so as to confirm they don't merely display their own hypocrisy. Why proclaim a lie?

It is in this sense that James refers to "faith alone"—a mere intellectual assent rather than legitimate saving faith. In Roman Catholicism intellectual assent *is* saving faith: that is, intellectual assent to the doctrines of the Church. But what proves our faith true is how we live and what we do, not merely a *claim* to faith in Christ or a church belief.

Again, in this sense good works may be said to justify us. Our faith is shown to be real—that is, it is vindicated or justified—by what we do. It cannot be vindicated or justified in any other manner. As James says, "You see that a person is justified by what he does and not by faith alone"—not by a *dead* faith (2:24). The true test of saving faith is obedience, not mere profession. Millions of people in both the Catholic and Protestant church profess faith—but how many really live for Christ?

Martin Luther correctly stated that justification *is* by faith alone, but *not* by the faith that is alone. Again, faith alone saves, but true faith inevitably leads to good works. James never even hints at salvation by law-keeping or by faith *and* works; he only demonstrates what true faith is and does. James vindicates true faith in the same manner that Paul vindicates true justification. James proves that true faith results in good works, while Paul proves that true faith alone justifies one before God. Both the apostle Paul and the apostle James agree on the nature of saving faith.

11

WHAT DOES ROMAN CATHOLICISM TEACH ABOUT THE DOCTRINES OF SALVATION AND JUSTIFICATION?

Catholicism is adamant that it does *not* teach salvation by works. And no one denies that Rome officially rejects salvation *solely* by works. After all, it agreed upon the condemnation of Pelagius (a monk who taught that man could lead a sin-free life without God's help) at the Synod of Carthage in A.D. 418 and ratified this position at the Council of Trent.

However, Rome's official condemnation of salvation by works *alone* confuses the issue. Rome may have officially condemned salvation *solely* by works, but it has also officially endorsed salvation by grace *and* works to such a degree that one does not enter heaven without individual works of righteousness and a great deal of earned personal merit.

Here is an illustration: You must try to run a 1,000-mile race over treacherous territory, with literally everything at stake, even your life. And here are the rules: You have to carry a 100-pound backpack and run without stopping. There are no water breaks, and every mile has to be a four-minute mile. Rome says that God's grace gets you in shape, but you have to run the race and finish the course to win. If you don't make it, you lose forever. Biblically, though, no one is in good enough shape to even enter the race, let alone run it, so God had Christ enter and run the race for you—

flawlessly, in world record time. The one who trusts in Christ wins forever because personal performance is not the issue: letting Christ take your place is.

True enough, the Catholic Church has always claimed that justification occurs by an act of God's grace. But where Rome's doctrine contradicts the biblical doctrine of justification is where it teaches that there are *two* aspects of justification—one by an act of grace, the other necessitating works. Without the latter, there is no justification. In other words, Protestants have only half a doctrine of justification, not actual justification at all. For both parties it's the difference between a bowl of salt for breakfast...or steak and eggs. And it truly is the difference between heaven and hell.

What Catholic Authorities Say

In this chapter we will cite two leading authorities for Catholic doctrine: the Council of Trent, convened to refute the alleged errors of the Protestant Reformation; and the *Catechism of the Catholic Church* (1994), the first official statement of Catholic teaching issued since the 1566 Catechism. In the introduction to the 1994 Catechism, John Paul II affirms its authority in Catholic doctrine:

> I declare it to be a *sure norm* for teaching the faith. This catechism is given to them [Catholic leaders and laity] that it may be a sure and authentic reference text for teaching *catholic doctrine.*...[It] is offered to every individual who wants to know what the Catholic Church believes.[1]

The 1994 Catechism

In the new catechism, the above-mentioned dual aspect of justification is clearly seen. The first aspect of justification occurs when man is moved by God to turn from sin; the second aspect of justification occurs as man progresses in good works and *merits* for himself the graces needed to attain eternal life:

Like conversion, justification has two aspects. Moved by grace, man turns toward God and away from sin [first aspect], and so accepts forgiveness and righteousness from on high. No one can merit the initial grace which is at the origin of conversion. [But once] moved by the Holy Spirit [first aspect] we can merit for ourselves [second aspect] and for others all the graces needed to attain eternal life.[2]

This is why the Pope is adamant that "man is justified by works and not by faith alone."[3]

This two-aspect definition allows Roman Catholic theologians to sound perfectly biblical about justification when they are talking about only phase one. The problem is, they are not talking about the Catholic concept of justification in its actual entirety.

The Council of Trent (1545–1564):

Keep in mind that the purpose of the Council of Trent was to reaffirm Catholic doctrine in reply to the alleged heresies of the Reformation begun by the Catholic priest and reformer, Martin Luther. Trent decreed clearly that man is saved by good works and that such good works merit reward from God:

- "By his good works the justified man really acquires a claim to supernatural reward from God."[4]

- "It is both possible and necessary to keep the law of God."[5]

- "But no one, however much justified, should consider himself exempt from the observance of the commandments."[6]

- "If anyone says that the sinner is justified by faith alone, meaning that nothing else is required to cooperate in order to obtain the grace of justification, let him be anathema."[7] (According to Webster, an *anathema* is "a ban or curse solemnly pronounced by ecclesiastical [church] authority and accompanied by excommunication.")

- For him who believes in "faith alone, but not…the observance of the whole law of Christ, let him be anathema."[8]

- Trent further decreed that heaven itself was a reward for those who do good works: "If anyone says that the good works of the one justified…are not also the good merits of him justified; or that the one justified…does not truly merit an increase of grace, eternal life, and in case he dies in grace, the attainment of eternal life itself and also an increase of glory, let him be anathema."[9]

The above statements and many more are proof that the Catholic Church actually teaches salvation by good works and personal merit. Only this can explain why the great majority of Catholic priests teach that salvation *is* by good works. Despite some recent changes in Catholicism, most priests remain loyal to Rome and this shows why, according to one of the most comprehensive polls of American clergy ever made, 75 to 80 percent of priests openly oppose the biblical gospel. (The good news here is that 20 to 25 percent apparently do not, a massive change since Trent.)

> Over three-quarters of Roman Catholic priests reject the view that our only hope for heaven is through personal faith in Jesus Christ as Lord and Savior. They hold instead that "heaven is a divine reward for those who earn it by their good life."

Priestly loyalty to Rome, that is, the Pope, also reveals why "four-fifths of all priests reject the Bible as the first place to turn in deciding religious questions; rather, they test their religious beliefs by what the Church says."[10]

12

IS SALVATION THROUGH ACCEPTING CATHOLIC BELIEFS?

The decrees of Trent, Vatican I, and Vatican II, as well as papal decrees (for example, concerning Mary) constitute part of the doctrinal content of true or saving faith. In order to be saved to heaven, one must believe them. All who disagree with or reject these teachings are *anathematized*. Practically, this means being cut off from the true Church, which alone possesses salvation. Remaining outside the Church—refusing personal repentance and return to the Church to embrace its teachings—results in condemnation to eternal hell.

In sum, the way to heaven is to accept whatever the Roman Catholic Church teaches—apart from this there is no salvation.

> To reject anything taught by the Roman church is to reject saving faith and to forfeit justification and eternal life [as declared in Vatican I]: "Further, all those things are to be believed with divine and Catholic faith which are contained in the word of God, written or handed down, and which the church, either by a solemn judgment or by her ordinary and universal magisterium, proposes for belief as having been divinely revealed....Nor will anyone obtain eternal life unless he shall have persevered in faith unto the end."
>
> A Catholic must believe with divine faith the whole of revelation, which is contained in the written word of God and in Sacred Tradition.

45. Can a person be a Catholic if he believes most, but not all, the teachings of revelation?

A person cannot be a Catholic if he rejects even a single teaching that he knows has been revealed by God.

46. What will happen to those who lack "the faith necessary for salvation"?

Those will not be saved who lack the necessary faith because of their own sinful neglect or conduct. As Christ declared, "He who does not believe will be condemned" (Mark 16:16).[1]

13

DO CATHOLICS AND PROTESTANTS MEAN THE SAME THINGS BY THE WORDS THEY USE?

The reason the majority of Catholic priests reject the biblical doctrine of salvation (as we saw in question 11) is because as priests—loyal to the Pope—they are required to reject the idea that divine authority resides only in the Bible. For them, divine authority resides in the Catholic Church and its Tradition, which alone properly interpret the Bible. Priests, therefore, look primarily to the Church for answers to religious questions because they believe only the Catholic Church can infallibly determine proper doctrine through its "divinely guided" interpretation of the Bible.

A study of Catholic history will show that it is the Church, and not the Bible, which has developed Catholic doctrine over the years. These doctrines are, in part, upheld by the unique definition Rome gives to biblical words. But the question is, "Are these words properly defined in their biblical sense?"

In chapter 6 of *Alice in Wonderland,* Lewis Carroll illustrated the problem:

> "When I use a word," Humpty Dumpty said, in a rather scornful tone, "it means just what I choose it to mean—neither more nor less." "The question is," said Alice, "whether you *can* make words mean so many different things." "The question is," said Humpty Dumpty, "which is to be the master—that's all…When I make a word do a lot of work…I always pay it extra."

As lawyer and philosopher Dr. John Warwick Montgomery pointed out in *The Shape of the Past,* words require specific definition by the user. When words are not defined properly, various problems are created.[1]

Both Protestants and Catholics use the same words, but mean entirely different things.[2] Protestants define words according to the biblical meaning, while Catholics change those meanings based on Church Tradition. This is true for words such as *grace, salvation, reconciliation, regeneration,* and *justification.* It is hardly surprising that the end result is confusion. Catholics themselves frequently acknowledge that their interpretation of biblical words differs from that of Reformation Protestantism. For example, *The Papal Encyclicals* agree that the word "faith has different meanings for a Catholic and a Protestant."[3] Keating is entirely correct when he points out, "As in so many matters, fundamentalists [for example, conservative Christians] and Catholics are at logger-heads because they define terms differently."[4]

Devout Catholics do not question their church's teaching about the definition of biblical terms because the Catholic Church believes that "over the Book [Bible] stands the Church."[5] The Church has final authority over the Bible, and therefore, it is the Church's interpretation of biblical words that is authoritative. As Keating argues, "The Bible…is interpreted infallibly only by the teaching authority invested by Jesus in the Catholic Church."[6]

In the end, it is the Church's definition of biblical terms—not the biblical definition—that wins the day. *The Papal Encyclicals* correctly point out that Protestants turn to the Bible alone to determine whether or not a doctrine is true. However,

> This is just the reverse of the Catholic's approach to belief. As the Catholic sees it, he must accept God on God's terms and not his own. It is not for him to "judge" the divine message, but only to receive it. Since he receives it from a living, teaching organ, he does not have to puzzle over the meaning of the revelation because the ever-present living magisterium [teaching office] can tell him exactly what the doctrine intends.[7]

In conclusion, by allowing biblical words to be redefined through the lens of Catholic Tradition, the Church of Rome has distorted the gospel.

14

DOES THE BIBLE TEACH THAT, IN *THIS* LIFE, THERE IS A TRUE AND PERMANENT GUARANTEE OF ENTERING HEAVEN?

The topic of salvation is so crucial that no one should trust solely in what another person or any church claims; one should trust only what God has clearly spoken. This is one reason God tells us we are to study the Scriptures: "Be diligent to present yourself approved to God as a workman who does not need to be ashamed, accurately handling the word of truth" (2 Timothy 2:15 NASB). Ignorance of the Bible results in nothing less than ignorance about salvation.

Again, as we saw in question 7, the Bible declares that full salvation is *solely* and *entirely* by grace—it comes freely to any individual who simply places genuine trust in Jesus Christ for forgiveness of sins. Please read the following Scriptures carefully:

> It is by grace you have been saved, through faith—and this *not from yourselves,* it is the gift of God—not by works, so that no one can boast (Ephesians 2:8-9).

> All who believe…are justified *freely by his grace* through the redemption that came by Christ….A man is justified by faith *apart from observing the law*" (Romans 3:22,24,28).

> All the prophets testify about him [Jesus] that everyone who *believes* in him *receives forgiveness* of sins through his name (Acts 10:43).

> In him we *have redemption* through his blood, the forgiveness of sins, in accordance with the riches of God's grace (Ephesians 1:7).

> …Not having a righteousness of my own that comes from the law, but that which is through *faith* in Christ—the righteousness that comes from God and is *by faith* (Philippians 3:9).

Catholics (by virtue of Church teaching), and many Protestants also (by virtue of poor teaching), have no assurance or certainty of their own salvation. With all that is at stake, that's not good. Further, Catholics in general—and even many evangelical Protestants—reject the doctrine of eternal security (that the true believer in Christ can never lose his or her salvation).

But not only does God want us to *know* that we can have the assurance of salvation in this life, but He also wants us to know that we will *never* be lost, even though the Catholic Church teaches that justification can be forfeited through the commission of mortal sin and the believer can go to hell forever.[1]

When Christ paid the full divine penalty for our sins 2,000 years ago, all our sins were in the future. If the Bible teaches that our sins are forgiven at the point of true faith in Christ, this must logically include all of them, even all future sins. "He forgave us *all* our sins" (Colossians 2:13). Therefore, come what may in life (please read Romans 8:28-39), the person who trusts in Christ alone for salvation will go to heaven when he dies because God Himself informs the believer that he or she now possesses "an inheritance that can never perish, spoil or fade" because it is "kept in heaven for you" (1 Peter 1:4). The salvation God offers is perfectly secure precisely *because* it involves His gracious act and is in no way dependent upon human merit or good works for its accomplishment. It is simply a *free gift* (Romans 3:24).

Because salvation occurs by God's grace and is in no way dependent upon anything we do to earn it, and because the divine penalty for all sin was fully paid by Jesus Christ on the cross, the Bible teaches that those who have genuinely received Christ as their personal Savior and Lord may from that point forward be *fully* assured that they *now* possess eternal life. Consider the following Scriptures very carefully:

> I *tell you the truth,* whoever hears my word and believes him who sent me *has eternal life* and will *not* be condemned; he *has* crossed over from death to life (John 5:24).

> *I tell you the truth,* he who believes *has everlasting life* (John 6:47).

> I write these things to you who *believe* in the name of the Son of God *so that* you may **know** that you *have eternal life* (1 John 5:13).

If any person currently possesses eternal life, can it be lost at any point in time...even in a thousand lifetimes?

15

WHAT ARE SOME PERSONAL CONSEQUENCES OF CATHOLIC THEOLOGY?

Catholicism teaches that a right standing before God is something that does not fully come about in this life, nor can it occur in a moment of time. It is something that comprises a lengthy process, earned only after a lifetime of good works and obtained merit and completed through torment in purgatory after death.

Catholics agree that, if a Catholic man or woman were to die today, he or she would have no assurance of going to heaven. As a 23-year Catholic recalled,

> In the Catholic Church I...had no assurance of my salvation because, as a Catholic, my salvation depended on the Sacraments of the church, the intermediation of Mary and the saints, and the forgiveness of God rested upon the priest through the confessional and the Sacrifice of the Mass. I did not realize the free gift of the Almighty God in Jesus Christ by faith alone.[1]

Throughout his life, the late evangelical authority Dr. Walter Martin had many conversations with individual Catholics and Catholic priests. In one of his books he discusses the scriptural proof that the believer in Christ has peace with God *now* (for example, Romans 5:1: "Having been justified by faith, we *have* peace with God through our Lord Jesus Christ"—NASB). He then says,

> No Roman Catholic who really believes the teachings of his Church has that peace with God….If you ask any Roman Catholic, "Do you know that God has completely forgiven you of your sins? Do you know that because Christ died in your place, as the Bible says, you have eternal salvation now? Do you know, right at this moment, that you have passed from death to life?" the answer is negative. Every Roman Catholic whom I have ever spoken to on this subject, be he priest, theologian or layman, has said to me, "I hope I will be saved; I truly hope so."[2]

A justification that is lost every time a mortal sin is committed cannot provide any security of salvation. Further, the Catholic Church teaches that mortal sins are common occurrences: envy, drunkenness, failure to attend Mass, using birth control, and so on.[3]

Worse, someone may have lived a perfect life in Catholicism for 70 years, and at the very moment of death—by one small omission—still go to an eternal hell: "The apparent saint can throw away salvation at the last moment and end up no better off than the man who never did a good deed in his life….Dying is by far one's most important act."[4]

In Catholicism the specific condition of the soul at the moment of death determines one's subsequent destiny. Given the weakness of faith and the commonness of mortal sin, when confronted by the immense power of "the world, the flesh, and the devil," who can possibly know the future condition of their dying—whether it will be favorable to salvation? Death is no reliable friend— it can come unexpected, in a flash, at an unguarded moment. Who then can ever know that their dying moments will arrive with goodwill rather than hostility?

Assurance Is Impossible

In *Catholicism and Fundamentalism*, Karl Keating emphasizes that, in Catholicism, men and women learn they will merit heaven by their good works and personal righteousness, but that to merely "accept Jesus" as Savior will accomplish nothing.

> For Catholics, salvation depends on the state of the soul at death. Christ...did his part, and now we have to cooperate by doing ours. If we are to pass through those [heavenly] gates, we have to be in the right spiritual state....The Church teaches that only souls that are objectively good and objectively pleasing to God merit heaven, and such souls are ones filled with sanctifying grace....As Catholics see it, anyone can achieve heaven, and anyone can lose it.
>   ..."Accepting Jesus" has nothing to do with turning a spiritually dead soul into a soul alive with sanctifying grace. The soul [that "accepts Jesus"] remains the same [that is, spiritually dead].[5]

In *My Ticket to Heaven,* a popular Catholic tract that has apparently sold some 10 million copies, readers are told that their "ticket to heaven" is good works and permanently abstaining from mortal sin. Thus, "If I do my part, God will do His part."[6] This booklet is labeled as "a Tract of Justification" and a "straightforward presentation of Christian faith," but its principal effect is to produce the fear of never achieving heaven—since justification is so clearly laid out as involving a practical perfection. Although written by a priest of 40 years, this tract never once mentions personal faith in Jesus Christ as the basis for salvation. No one can possibly do what this booklet says they must do in order to maintain and increase their justification so that they will go to heaven. Compare this small booklet to the libraries of Rome's canon law and you witness the fruit of despair.

In Catholicism, the requirements for even relative "assurance" of salvation are saving faith, loyal membership in the Church, obedience to the commandments, love of God and neighbor, and participation in the sacraments of the Eucharist, penance, and so on—plus prayer, good works, indulgences and, last but certainly not least, persevering in God's grace until death and, at the point of death, dying in the right condition.[7]

This is not the assurance that God declares for believers in Scripture:

> Since we *have now been justified* by his blood, how much *more* shall we be *saved from God's wrath* through him! For if, when we were God's enemies, we were reconciled to him through the death of his Son, *how much more, having been reconciled,* shall we *be saved* through his life! (Romans 5:9-10).

> If God is for us, *who can be against us?* He who did not spare his own Son, but gave him up for us all—how will he not also, along with him, graciously give us all things? Who will bring any charge against those whom God has chosen? *It is God who justifies.* Who is he that condemns? (Romans 8:31-34).

> I am *convinced* that neither death nor life, neither angels nor demons, neither the present nor the future, nor any powers, neither height nor depth, or *anything else in all creation,* will be able to separate us from the love of God that is in Christ Jesus our Lord (Romans 8:38-39).

No one needs to be tormented over his or her relationship to God, as many today are. Anyone can immediately have rest and be assured that God has declared full pardon for him or her from all the penalty due his or her sins. Genuine trust in Christ results in full peace with God—and that's the gospel (John 6:47; Romans 5:1,9-11; 1 John 5:13).

Roman Catholic Practices

16

What Are the Seven Sacraments?

*The fact that Christianity is a religion of salvation is
expressed in the sacramental life of the Church....
Baptism and the Eucharist [are] sacraments which
create in man the seed of eternal life.*

—Pope John Paul II[1]

In contrast to Protestantism, which accepts the two scriptural
sacraments (baptism and communion), Roman Catholicism
teaches there are seven *sacraments*—rites that are believed to
grant divine grace. It believes all these were instituted by Jesus
Christ solely on the basis that they were instituted by the Catholic
Church. The sacraments of Catholicism involve particular spiritual activities or responsibilities partaken of by church members,
and the seven are baptism, the Holy Eucharist, penance, matrimony, anointing of the sick, confirmation, and holy orders.

The alleged results of each of the sacraments may be summarized as follows:

1. *Baptism* as an infant (not repeated) cleanses from original sin, removes other sin and its punishment, provides
   justification in an initial form, provides spiritual rebirth

(John 3:3) or regeneration, and is "necessary for salva-tion."[2]

2. *Confirmation* (not repeated) bestows the Holy Spirit in a special sense, leading to "an increase of sanctifying grace and the gifts of the Holy Spirit" as well as other spiritual power and a sealing to the Catholic Church. Confirma-tion gives strength from the Holy Spirit to defend the Catholic faith and to avoid temptation. (In a sense, the larger process of justification begins at confirmation because justification cannot begin prior to faith, which is defined as "man's assent to revealed [that is, Catholic] truth," nor can it occur before baptism.)[3]

3. *Penance* (or reconciliation) removes the penalty of sins committed after baptism and confirmation. Mortal, or "deadly," sins are remitted and the "justification" lost by such sins is restored as a continuing process. Penance is a particular act or acts considered as satisfaction offered to God in reparation for sin committed. According to *The Catholic Encyclopedia,* Jesus Christ Himself insti-tuted the sacrament of penance for "the pardon of sins committed after baptism." Thus, "In the sacrament of penance, the faithful obtain from the mercy of God pardon for their sins against Him...."[4]*

4. *Holy Eucharist* comprises Christ's being "re-sacrificed," or re-presented, through which the benefits of Calvary are continually applied anew to the believer.[5] This occurs at the Mass, wherein the bread and wine literally become Christ through the alleged miracle termed *transubstanti-ation.*

---

* A popular Catholic version of the Bible, the Douay–Rheims, even translates the text at var-ious places to support the concept of penance by replacing the word *repentance* with *penance*—despite these concepts involving two entirely different things. For example: "No, I say to you: but unless you shall do penance, you shall all likewise perish" (Luke 13:3 DRV).

5. *Marriage.* Grace is given to remain in the bonds of matrimony in accordance with the requirements of the Catholic Church.[6]

6. *Anointing of the sick* (formerly *extreme unction*) bestows grace on those who are sick, old, or near death and helps in forgiveness of sins and sometimes the physical healing of the body.[7]

7. *Holy orders* (not repeated) confers special grace and spiritual power upon bishops, priests, and deacons for leadership in the Church as representatives of Christ "for all eternity": "Holy Orders is the Sacrament of the New Law instituted by Christ, through which spiritual power is given together with the grace to exercise properly the respective office. The sacrament gives a permanent character, meaning that it cannot be repeated, and that it ordains one for all eternity."[8]

This sevenfold sacramental system was not initiated until the twelfth century and was not made a permanent part of the Catholic faith until as late as the fifteenth century. This means that for more than 1,000 years Catholics were not required to accept the current sacramental system. Nevertheless, for today's Roman Catholic, "His whole life from the cradle to the grave, and indeed beyond the grave in purgatory, is conditioned by the sacramental approach."[9] The 1994 Catechism emphasizes the crucial importance of the sacraments for the Catholic believer when it declares, "The whole liturgical life of the Church revolves around the Eucharistic sacrifice and the sacraments."[10]

17

What Is the Alleged Power of the Sacraments?

The sacraments are presided over by a Catholic priest who acts as a mediator between God and man. Here are the words of Pope

Paul VI in his September 3, 1965, encyclical,* *Mysterium Fidei* ("Mystery of Faith"):

> No one is unaware that the sacraments are the actions of Christ, who administers them through men. Therefore, the sacraments are holy in themselves, and by the power of Christ they pour grace into the soul when they touch the body.[1]

In essence, the sacraments purportedly allow the church member the specific means, through specific works of merit, to maintain his or her justification, increase it, and finally attain heaven. These special activities are said to dispense God's grace (the word *grace* here is used to mean a spiritual substance or power) and God's favor.

What Catholicism offers its one billion members is, in effect, a *priestly,* or *sacerdotal,* religion. In such a system, salvation is mediated through the functions of the priesthood (in this case through the Catholic sacraments). Only Catholic priests and those above them can perform the sacraments—so in effect, these individuals hold the keys to salvation.

Even though the Church declares that it is Christ who performs the sacraments and dispenses grace in the life of the believer (through the priest), and therefore the effects of the sacrament are supposedly not produced by the righteousness of the believer, it is nevertheless the believer's responsibility to accept or perform the sacraments. This is said to instill more grace and more righteousness as an ongoing process. Church members must be baptized, confirmed, partake of the Eucharist, do penance, and so on if they are to increase their personal righteousness to merit salvation.

If the believer does not do these things, he simply cannot be saved. At this point the sacraments function as a powerful tether to the Catholic Church. The 1994 Catechism unequivocally states,

---

* Encyclicals are circular letters to the bishops given for the welfare of the church; the best-known and most controversial is that of Paul VI, *Humanae Vitae* (1968), on birth control.

"The Church affirms that for believers the sacraments of the New Covenant are necessary for salvation."[2] A standard Catholic text, *Fundamentals of Catholic Dogma,* while conceding that God can in some extreme circumstances communicate grace without the sacraments, nevertheless asserts,

> The sacraments of the New Covenant are necessary for the salvation of mankind....The sacraments are the means appointed by God for the attainment of eternal salvation. Three of them [baptism, penance, Holy Orders] are in the ordinary way of salvation so necessary that without their use salvation cannot be attained.[3]

Rather than assist even a relative "assurance" of salvation, the sacraments work against any form of assurance. Again, if forgiveness of sins and final salvation depend on what we do and achieve as a lifelong process through the sacraments, how can we possibly know that our performance will be properly maintained until the end?

"Ex Opere Operato"?

The sacraments are said to "work by their own working" to "confer grace to the soul." The 1994 Catechism puts it this way: "The sacraments act *ex opere operato*"[4]—literally, "by the very fact of the action's being performed."

In brief, the sacraments are believed to be effective in dispensing divine grace as a substance or power to the individual Catholic when he partakes of each specific sacrament. Through the sacraments, "internal grace is that received in the interior of the soul, enabling us to act supernaturally." Further, "the supernatural gift of God infused into the very essence of the soul as a habit is habitual grace. This grace is also called sanctifying or justifying grace, because it is included in both."[5] In essence, "the soul becomes good and holy through the infusion of grace" in the sacraments.[6] This allegedly increases one's justification.

But is there real evidence that the sacraments dispense supernatural power to live holy lives? Then what of the many scandals throughout church history among the Popes, for example?

Consider further how many, perhaps most, individual Catholics seem to have lived their lives. Emmett McLoughlin, a disillusioned priest who eventually turned to liberal Protestantism, wrote a book in which he cited statistics to document that, in its most important work—producing morality—the Catholic Church "is a failure. Among its members crime and immorality are greater than among the unchurched or the members of other churches."[7] If the Catholic sacraments worked automatically, none of this should be true.

18

HOW DO CATHOLIC AND PROTESTANT VIEWS OF THE SACRAMENTS DIFFER?

The real difference between the Protestant and Catholic view of sacraments is not in their number: two versus seven. Rather, it is in what the sacraments are believed to do—in their meaning and purpose.

Protestantism sees both baptism and communion primarily as symbols and memorials of vital theological truths. Baptism, for example, symbolizes the believer's death to his old life and resurrection to new life in Jesus Christ (Romans 6:1-13). Communion commemorates the death of Christ for our sins and also reminds the believer that not only did Christ die for all the believer's sins (Colossians 2:13), but that He also rose from the dead as proof of the believer's justification before God (Romans 4:25).

But Catholicism sees the sacraments as actually changing a person inwardly, through a continual form of regeneration, justification, and spiritual empowerment. This explains why the basis for the doctrine of justification in Catholic theology is not the fact of Christ's righteousness being imputed (transferred or credited) once for all to a believer solely by faith. Rather, it is that—through the sacraments—Christ's righteousness is infused into one's very being (initial justification) so that a person progressively becomes more and more righteous. And on that basis—the fact one progresses in actual outward righteousness—one is eventually declared righteous, and then after death and time in purgatory one becomes "ultimately righteous." Thus, we again see that in Catholicism final justification occurs primarily by means of the sacraments and progressive spiritual growth—not by faith alone.

In 1547 the Council of Trent decreed the following concerning the sacraments:

> Wherefore, in order to destroy the errors and extirpate the heresies that in our stormy times are directed against the most holy sacraments…which are exceedingly detrimental to the purity of the Catholic Church and the salvation of souls, the holy ecumenical and general Council of Trent…has thought it proper to establish and enact these present canons.[1]

The canons include numerous declarations that sacraments are necessary for salvation. And the declarations are given for the sacraments as a whole and for each individual sacrament. For example:

- Canons 3 and 6 relate to the Mass: "If anyone says that the sacrifice of the Mass is one only of praise and thanksgiving; or that it is a mere commemoration of sacrifice consummated on the cross but not a propitiatory one; or that it profits him only who receives, and ought not to be offered for the living and the dead, for sins, punishments, satisfactions, and other necessities, let him be anathema." "If anyone says that the canon of the Mass contains errors and is therefore to be abrogated, let him be anathema."[2]

- Canon 4 reads, "If anyone says that the sacraments...are not necessary for salvation...and that without the desire of them men obtain from God through faith alone the grace of justification...let him be anathema."[3]

As Catholic theologian Ludwig Ott says, for the Catholic, "eternal blessedness in heaven is the reward for good works performed on this earth."[4] Indeed, unless these are maintained throughout life, a Catholic, irrespective of his faith in Christ, can still go to hell forever.

The Problem of the Sacraments

In the end, for Catholicism it is still *my* work and *my* merit that makes it possible for God to restore me to the process of justification and salvation in order to earn the right to heaven. The sacraments are something *I* perform in order to keep me out of hell. But throughout the New Testament it is the merit of Jesus Christ *alone* that reconciles us, justifies us, redeems us, saves us, and assures our entrance into heaven—nothing we do at all.

The Catholic sacraments are a constant reminder and demand for works that must be performed in order to finally merit heaven after death. The biblical doctrine of justification cancels this view by teaching that the believer can *know* he has a perfect standing with God and the assurance of heaven the moment he places his total faith in Christ to save him.

Justification is not progressive. It happens instantaneously and eternally at the point of true faith in Jesus Christ. *That's* the glory of the gospel.

19

WHAT IS THE MASS?

The Mass is the most important sacrament because of what it is believed to accomplish. Roman Catholicism teaches that the sacrifice of Jesus Christ Himself is actually re-presented to the faithful and its benefits are applied to them. Because of this sacri-ficing of Jesus in every Mass, God's wrath against sin is presently appeased. Though not a re-crucifixion on the cross, it *is* a literal *re-sacrificing* of Christ:

> Christ is not dying all over again. What is on the altar is the *very same sacrifice* as on Calvary, but it is made present to us today in a special, sacramental way. This is a presence distinct from a physical, historical presence and distinct from a merely symbolical presence. It is a third kind of presence. In it *Christ is really present on the altar,* and at the consecration a *real offering of Christ* to the Father is made.[1]

Indeed, if the blessings of Christ occur through the Mass, then those who do not partake of the Mass are without those blessings and will suffer the appropriate consequences.

The 1994 Catechism describes the Mass as "the source and summit of the Christian life"; "the sum and summary of our faith"; and "the Sacrament of sacraments."[2] Here we find Rome's doctrine of *transubstantiation*—that the bread and wine each lit-erally *become* the body and blood of the Lord Jesus Christ, meaning that Christ *is* upon the altar as the sacrificial victim, to be offered up as a living sacrifice to propitiate God's wrath against sin. Thus, "it is by the conversion of the bread and wine into Christ's body and blood that Christ becomes present in this sacra-ment," and "in the most blessed sacrament of the Eucharist...the whole Christ is truly, really and substantially contained."[3] The Catholic Church believes that all of Christ, blood and body, is pre-sent in both the bread and wine. Therefore, even though usually only the priest is allowed to partake of the wine, the layman nev-ertheless partakes of Christ's blood through partaking of the bread.[4]

Furthermore, because Christ is quite literally present in His entirety in the Eucharist, the Catholic Church believes that the Eucharist should be worshiped, or *venerated.* This is why priests and Catholics *genuflect* (bend the knee) when the host is pre-sent—because it is really *Christ* present.

The Catholic Church has always offered and still offers to the sacrament of the Eucharist the cult of adoration [worship], not only during Mass, but also outside of it, reserving the consecrated hosts with the utmost care, exposing them to the solemn veneration of the faithful, and carrying them in procession.[5]

As the Council of Trent declared,

THE BLESSED SACRAMENT IS OUR LORD AND MUST BE WORSHIPPED: If anyone says that in the holy sacrament of the Eucharist the only-begotten Son of God is not to be adored even outwardly with the worship of latria [worship due God alone]... let him be anathema.[6]

The doctrine of transubstantiation was codified in its present form by Thomas Aquinas (1225–1274). Nevertheless, this doctrine cannot be established biblically. *Belief* in Jesus is the metaphorical equivalent of "eating" His flesh and blood (John 6:35-36). In other words, Jesus was telling His disciples to spiritually (not physically) receive Him—ingest and digest Him—and His teachings—not to eat His literal physical flesh and blood.

The Benefits of the Mass

The following statements from the 1994 Catechism (which cites various authoritative sources) show in what manner the blessings of Christ's death are thought to be applied to believers during the Mass. These reveal that participation in the Eucharist is also part of the process of justification:

The sacrifice of Christ and the sacrifice of the Eucharist are one single sacrifice....."In this divine sacrifice which is celebrated in the Mass, the same Christ who offered himself once in a bloody manner on the altar of the cross is contained and is offered in an unbloody manner."[7]

The Eucharistic sacrifice is also offered for *the faithful departed* [in purgatory] who "have died in Christ but are not yet wholly purified," so that they may be able to enter into the light and peace of Christ.[8]

Holy Communion…*preserves, increases, and renews the life of grace received at Baptism.*…The Eucharist cannot unite us to Christ without at the same time cleansing us from past sins and preserving us from future sins.…[It] *wipes away venial sins.*…The Eucharist *preserves us from future mortal sins.*[9]

In sum, the Mass is believed to 1) re-sacrifice Christ and apply the benefits of the cross to believers; 2) carry out the work of redemption; 3) forgive sin; 4) help purify those in purgatory; 5) increase the life of grace received at baptism; 6) cleanse from past sins and sanctify or preserve from future sins—even mortal ones; and 7) pour out the grace of salvation upon all the Church.[10]

Once for All

Who can deny that participation in the Mass is necessary for salvation—and is also therefore a form of salvation by works? Doesn't this remind us of the ancient Hebrew sacrificial system with its required repetition of sacrifices year after year that were perpetual reminders of sins? Isn't that why Jesus died, to do away with the old system?

The Catholic Church can only derive all of these teachings from its Tradition because Scripture rejects this view through its teaching of a *once-for-all* atonement for sin and its penalty:

Where there is forgiveness of these things, there is *no longer any offering* for sin (Hebrews 10:18 NASB).

He [Jesus] sacrificed for their sins *once for all* when he offered himself.… He entered the Most Holy Place *once for all* by his own blood, *having obtained eternal redemption* …[He] offered *for all time one sacrifice for sins*…because by *one sacrifice* he has made *perfect forever* those who are being made holy. The Holy Spirit also testifies to us about this....He says:..."Their sins and lawless acts I will remember no more" (Hebrews 7:27; 9:12; 10:12,14,15,17).

Let us consider how the above Scripture (Hebrews 9:12) is treated by Pope John Paul II in his book *Crossing the Threshold of Hope.* He writes, "Through the shedding of his own blood, Jesus Christ constantly 'enters into God's sanctuary thus obtaining eternal redemption' (cf. Hebrews 9:12)."[11]

First, Christ is not *continually* obtaining eternal redemption daily in the Mass; it was already obtained, once for all, 2,000 years ago at the cross. This is why translators render this verse as "having obtained eternal redemption." Second, the Greek word for "entered" is in the *aorist* tense, indicating a one-time past event, yet the Pope renders it in the present tense—"enters"—and even quotes this as Scripture. Third, the Pope replaces "once for all" with "constantly," altering the finality of the atonement. The Pope assumes the truth of Catholic doctrine and adjusts Scripture to conform with such teaching.

20

HOW DOES THE MASS IMPACT CHRIST'S ATONEMENT?

Rome holds that the Mass in no way detracts from the atonement of Christ. But is this true? The Mass itself, because of Rome's belief in Christ's actual presence in the wine and host, is defined throughout Catholicism as being "truly propitiatory." In other words, it literally forgives sins. Because the Mass pardons sins, it is held to be necessary for salvation.

Catholics and Protestants agree that sin is an affront to God's holiness, calling forth God's just condemnation. They agree that a propitiation is an offering made to God in light of His offended justice so that He becomes favorable toward the sinner. But Protestants disagree with the following: "Hence the Mass as a propitiation is offered to effect the remission of sins."[1]

Instead of Christ's once-for-all offering at Calvary being sufficient for forgiveness, the Council of Trent upholds the view that the Mass is required to forgive sin: "This sacrifice [of the Mass] is truly propitiatory....For by this oblation the Lord is appeased...and he pardons wrongdoing and sins, even grave ones."[2] The *Fundamentals of Catholic Dogma* states, "In the Sacrifice of the Mass, Christ's Sacrifice on the cross is made present, its memory is celebrated, and its saving power is applied," and, "As a propitiatory sacrifice the Sacrifice of the Mass effects the remission of sins and the punishment of sins."[3]

The Catholic Church has always emphasized the fact that Christ is re-sacrificed in the Mass (Catholics use the term *re-presented*) as a propitiation to God. Trent affirmed that the sacrifice of the Mass is propitiatory both for the living and even the dead because it offers "in an unbloody manner *the same Christ* who once offered Himself in a bloody manner on the altar of the cross," and therefore

> it is rightly offered not only for the sins, punishments, satisfactions and other necessities of the faithful who are living, but also for those departed in Christ, but not yet fully purified [that is, those in purgatory].[4]

Pope Pius XII, in his 1947 encyclical *Mediator Dei*, reaffirmed the Council of Trent when he stressed that the sacrifice of the Mass was not a "mere commemoration" of the passion and death of Christ, as Protestants teach, but

> is truly and properly the offering of a sacrifice wherein by an unbloody immolation [something offered as a sacrifice], the High Priest does what He [Jesus] had already done on the Cross, offering Himself to the Eternal Father as a most acceptable victim.[5]

Vatican II continued this view of the Mass, also reaffirming the position of Trent: "One and the same is the victim, one and the same is He Who now offers by the ministry of His priests, and Who then offered Himself on the Cross; the difference is only in the manner of offering."[6] As a result, Vatican II teaches that, at the Mass, "the faithful gather, and find help and comfort through venerating the presence of the Son of God our Savior, offered for us on the sacrificial altar."[7]

According to Karl Keating in *Catholicism and Fundamentalism,* "the Church insists that the Mass is the continuation and representation of the sacrifice of Calvary."[8] Emphasizing that it is not a re-crucifixion of Christ in which Christ suffers and dies again, he cites John A. O'Brien: "The Mass is the renewal and perpetuation of the sacrifice of the Cross in the sense that it offers anew to God the Victim of Calvary...and applies the fruits of Christ's death upon the Cross to individual human souls."[9]

What this means is that Catholicism teaches that Christ is still offering Himself today in tens of thousands of Masses conducted regularly throughout the world.[10] We stress that here the Mass is not merely the symbolic offering of the Eucharist or the thanksgiving of the faithful. Instead, "it is the supreme moment in the Church's worship when the priest claims to offer Christ as a sacrifice for the living and the dead."[11]

Not one verse in the Bible supports this teaching, however. The Catholic Mass constitutes a rejection of the biblical teaching on the atonement.

21

What Is the Biblical Teaching on Christ's Atonement?

A continual re-sacrificing of Christ is not what we find taught in the Bible. Rather, Christ is pictured as having accomplished His work once and for all and having sat down at the right hand of the Father (Hebrews 1:3; 8:1). The finality of Christ's sacrifice stands in stark contrast with the Catholic concept of the constant "renewal" of that sacrifice in the Mass.

Consider the book of Hebrews. It repeatedly uses terms such as "once," "once for all," and "forever" to emphasize both the perfection and the finality of Christ's death on the cross (9:12,26,28; 10:12,14). If Christ offered one sacrifice for sins forever and thus obtained eternal redemption for us (9:12; 10:10-14), what is the need for a perpetual "bloodless sacrifice" of Christ over and over again, literally millions of times? How can the Mass apply a forgiveness of sins that was already fully earned by Christ on the cross and applied to the believer at the very point of saving faith (John 5:24; 6:47)?

The writer of Hebrews reminds every believer of what God Himself has personally told them: "Their sins and lawless acts I will remember no more." The writer then goes on to state, "And where these have been forgiven, there is no longer any sacrifice for sin" (Hebrews 10:17-18). If there is no longer a sacrifice for sin, what can possibly be the need for the Mass as a sacrifice for sin?

Catholicism teaches that, by participating in the Mass—through a specific sacramental act or work—the believer can actually help to forgive his own sin and maintain and increase his own "justification" (which, as we have seen, is for Catholics the progressive sanctification that finally merits eternal life). Clearly, this is another form of salvation by works. It is one reason Catholicism teaches that participation in the Eucharist is part of a whole system of progressive salvation that, in the end, actually *merits* heaven for the believer.

The Scripture Is Clear

In contrast, the Scripture is clear: "one sacrifice for sins forever"; "once for all"; "it is finished"; and so on (Romans 6:10; Hebrews 7:27; 9:26-28; 10:10-14; 1 Peter 3:18; John 19:30). Thus, in the book of Hebrews we are told that Christ was not to offer Himself repeatedly, for then He would have had to suffer repeatedly since the foundation of the world:

> Nor did he enter heaven *to offer himself again and again*, the way the high priest enters the Most Holy Place every

year with blood that is not his own. Then Christ would have had to suffer many times since the creation of the world. But now he has appeared *once for all* at the end of the ages *to do away with sin* by the sacrifice of himself. Just as man is destined to die once, and after that to face judgment, so Christ *was sacrificed once* to take away the sins of many people; and he will appear a second time, not to bear sin, but to bring salvation to those who are waiting for him (Hebrews 9:25-28).

This final sacrifice is further contrasted with the Levitical priestly sacrifices, which "can never take away sins" (Hebrews 10:11). Indeed, it is the very repetition of the sacrifices that proves their insufficiency. Otherwise, they would "have ceased to be offered" (Hebrews 10:2 NASB). Then, "when [Christ] had offered *for all time one sacrifice for sins,* he sat down at the right hand of God...because by *one sacrifice* he has *made perfect forever* those who are being made holy" (Hebrews 10:12,14).

Jesus' perfect sacrifice, reflected by His own cry from the cross, "It is finished" (John 19:30), leaves no room for the Catholic re-sacrifice of Christ at the Mass or the idea that Christ is actually present in the bread and wine.

22

WHAT IS PENANCE?

The Catholic Church teaches that after baptism, if a man or woman commits mortal sin, he or she will lose his or her justification. In order to regain justification a person must perform the sacrament of *penance.*

According to *The Catholic Encyclopedia,* Jesus Christ Himself instituted the sacrament of penance for "the pardon of sins committed after baptism." Thus, "in the Sacrament of Penance, the faithful obtain from the mercy of God pardon for their sins against Him."[1]

Penance is a particular act or series of acts considered as satisfaction offered to God as a reparation for sin committed. Penance may involve what is known as *mortification,* or self-punishment, such as wearing an irritating shirt woven of coarse animal hair; prayer (for example, the Rosary); or a religious pilgrimage to a shrine of Christ or Mary; or any number of other deeds.[2]

As noted, the sacrament of penance is designed specifically to deal with sins committed after baptism. Why? Because the grace that is received or infused in baptism can be entirely lost by mortal ("deadly") sin. Mortal sin is held to be deadly because it literally destroys the grace of God within a person, making salvation necessary again. Thus, a new sacrament is necessary in order to restore an individual to the state of grace first received at baptism.

In fact, without penance a person *cannot* be restored to salvation. This is one reason why the Council of Trent actually referred to the sacrament of penance as a "second plank" of justification:

> Those who through sin have forfeited the received grace of justification, can again be justified when, moved by God, they exert themselves to obtain through the Sacrament of Penance the recovery, by the merits of Christ, of the grace lost. For this manner of justification is restoration for those fallen, which the holy Fathers have aptly called a second plank after the shipwreck of grace lost.[3]

As the 1994 Catechism emphasizes,

> Christ instituted the Sacrament of Penance for all sinful members of his church: above all for those who, since baptism, have fallen into grave sin, and have thus lost their baptismal grace. It is to them that the sacrament of Penance offers a new possibility to convert and to recover the grace of justification. The Fathers of the Church present this sacrament as "the second plank [of salvation] after the shipwreck which is the loss of grace."[4]

The Catechism teaches that God forgives sins through penance. After discussing different forms of penance in the Catholic life, such as fasting, prayer, almsgiving, the Eucharist, Scripture reading, praying the Liturgy of the Hours, praying the Our Father, and so on, it says this: "Every sincere act of worship or devotion revives the spirit of conversion and repentance within us and contributes to the forgiveness of our sins." Further, "the disclosure or confession of sins to a priest is an essential element of the sacrament."[5]

The sacrament of penance has three parts: first, *contrition*—a person must be sorry for his sins; second, *confession*—a person must fully confess each one of his mortal sins to a priest, as noted above; and third, *satisfaction*—a person must do works of piety such as fasting, saying prayers, almsgiving, or others that the priest gives him to do.

Complete spiritual health cannot be had apart from acts of penance: "Raised up from sin, the sinner must still recover his full spiritual health by doing something more to make amends for the sin: he must 'make satisfaction for' or 'expiate' his sins."[6]

Penance As a Form of Salvation

On the basis of what we have discussed, salvation through good works is evident in the doctrine of penance. As *The Catholic Encyclopedia* states,

> The result of mortal sin is the loss of sanctifying grace, the loss of the gifts of the Holy Spirit, remorse, and the punitive effect of *eternal separation from God*. To avoid these consequences, the reception of the Sacrament of Penance is required to return to the love of God.[7]

In other words, apart from performing the three parts of the sacrament of penance, a Catholic who commits mortal sin is immediately destined for eternal punishment in hell.

But none of this is biblical. Biblically, prior to salvation all sin is mortal. Even the smallest sin against God is sufficient to condemn a person eternally. But after salvation no sin is mortal, no matter how grave, because Christ paid the full divine penalty for every sin—small, large, or massive—on the cross. This complete forgiveness, God's pardon, has been freely given to the believer (Ephesians 1:7; Colossians 2:13).

Further, according to Scripture, salvation is based on God's grace—"not by works but by him who calls" (Romans 9:12). Salvation "does not, therefore, depend on man's desire or effort, but on God's mercy" (verse 16). If salvation is by grace, then it depends entirely on God. Therefore no saved person can ever be lost and no mortal sin can *ever* cancel a person's justification.

Catholics who believe their mortal sins are forgiven by the work of penance are being deceived concerning what the Bible really teaches. If Christ alone truly saves them, then their mortal sins—all of them—are already fully forgiven by the death of Christ solely through their faith in Jesus. No priestly confession or satisfaction is needed.

But if Catholics are *not* saved, then all the penance in the world cannot forgive their sins, whether such sins are "mortal" or the less serious "venial" ones. Biblically, it is Christ alone who forgives all our sins when we place our faith in Him.

23

WHAT ARE INDULGENCES?

The requirement that Catholics gain indulgences and undergo purgatory is another consequence of Rome's view of justification. Why? Justification is a lifelong process that may be increased, decreased, lost, regained, and so on—numerous times. Because Catholic salvation does not involve the full forgiveness of sins and a permanent pardon from all punishment, Rome has instituted various ways to solve these problems.

As we have discussed, Catholicism reinstates the allegedly lost justification, through penance, while indulgences and purgatory respectively remit and execute the temporal (noneternal) punishments for sin that are still thought necessary. The 1994 Catechism teaches the following: "The doctrine and practice of indulgences in the Church are closely linked to the effects of the Sacrament of Penance."[1] In other words, penance restores justification, while indulgences assist in removing punishment for subsequent sins. Indulgences are necessary because, when people sin, God's justice requires a punishment beyond that given to Christ on the cross.

In its practice of indulgences, Rome attempts to refrain from inflicting the temporal punishment due certain sins so that the Catholic will not have to suffer punishment. But Catholics are also told that, when they die, nearly all of them will have to suffer actual torment for their sins in purgatory.

What Indulgences Are and How They Work

Apologist Karl Keating informs Catholics they are in error if they think the Church has "dropped its old belief in indulgences"—which, incidentally, supposedly have the power to remove Catholics from purgatory more quickly. Further, he notes, "Many Catholics simply don't know what indulgences are."[2]

Indulgences are actions that assist in removing the punishment for sins. No one enjoys punishment, and the Catholic Church claims it has the power to prevent divine punishment for sins, another potent tether holding Catholics to their Church. Indulgences are gained through various acts of piety (such as saying the Rosary). These acts allegedly apply the merits of Christ and the earned merits of Mary and the Catholic saints (see below) to Catholic believers today—even to those allegedly in purgatory. This allows believers on earth and in purgatory to escape at least some of the punishment due their sins.[3] In other words, the *guilt* for sins may have been removed by the atonement of Christ and the sacraments, but all the *punishment* for them is not. "We can be forgiven [our sins], yet still have to suffer."[4]

The Catholic Encyclopedia explains the rationale for indulgences and the basis on which the Church offers them:

> The remission of the temporal punishment due for sins and hence, the satisfaction owed to God for one's sins is called an indulgence. Indulgences granted by the Church may be gained for oneself or for the souls in purgatory. The granting of indulgences is founded upon three doctrines of Catholic faith: the treasury of the merits of the communion of saints, Christ himself, and the Blessed Virgin and the saints.[5]

Because Christ, Mary, and the relatively small number of Catholic saints (less than 800 throughout Catholic history, the majority lately canonized by John Paul II)[6] have all provided "superabundant satisfactions" to God through their good works and righteousness, the Church believes it can offer these surplus merits to the Catholic believer to remit punishment. Rome claims that in granting indulgences it "dispenses and applies with authority the treasury of the satisfactions of Christ and the saints."[7] In sum, punishment for sin is canceled by the good deeds of Catholic saints, the Virgin Mary, and Jesus Christ, which are applied to the believer who performs the requirements of the indulgence.[8]

Types of Indulgences

There are two kinds of indulgences. First, those which are "easy" to gain (called *partial* indulgences); and second, those which are more difficult to obtain (called *plenary* indulgences). The difference concerns how much punishment for sin they allegedly remove. Plenary indulgences remove all temporal punishment due to sin, while partial indulgences only remove part of the punishment due to sin.[9] "This punishment [for sin] may come either in this life, in the form of various sufferings, or in the next life, in purgatory. We don't get rid of here [through indulgences] what we suffer there [in purgatory]."[10] In other words, any punishment for sin that is not remitted through indulgences in this life must then be endured in purgatory.

Luther on Indulgences

The great reformer Martin Luther would have none of this, because of what indulgences implied about the cross, and due to their ease of corruption. His famous Ninety-Five Theses (October 31, 1517) were written primarily against indulgences—the practices surrounding which had become extremely pernicious:

> There is no divine authority for preaching that the soul flies out of the purgatory immediately as the money clinks in the bottom of the chest (Number 27).

> All those who believe themselves certain of their own salvation by means of letters of indulgence, will be eternally damned, together with their teachers (Number 32).

> ...Surely this is a new sort of compassion, on the part of God and the Pope, when an impious man, an enemy of God, is allowed to pay money to redeem a devout soul, a friend of God; while yet that devout and beloved soul is not allowed to be redeemed without payment (Number 84).[11]

The modern Catholic Church maintains that, if a person ever bought an indulgence merely to get a soul out of purgatory or for forgiveness of sins, this was wrong. The Church also claims that it never officially condoned the massive abuses of the practice in earlier years. Regardless, it did clearly share in responsibility for them.

Indulgences Today

Today, making the sign of the cross, acts of devotion to Mary, and performing the Rosary are "highly indulgenced" by Rome:

> The faithful, as often as they devoutly sign themselves with the sign of the cross, are granted an indulgence of *three years;* whenever they make the same holy sign with blessed water, they may gain an indulgence of *seven years.*[12]

> One of the many indulgences attached to the devotion [of Mary] is that the faithful who recite the Rosary together in a family group, besides the partial indulgence of ten years, are granted a plenary indulgence twice a month, if they perform this recitation daily for a month, go to confession, receive Holy Communion, and visit some Church or public oratory.[13]

> Indulgences are also granted for visits of the faithful to various Catholic shrines, some of which were built in honor of Marian apparitions [alleged appearances by Mary].[14]

Indulgences are received only by performing the specific work or requirements to which the indulgence is attached. For example, three conditions are necessary to gain a plenary indulgence in addition to performing the specific requirements of that indulgence: sacramental confession, Eucharistic communion, and prayer for the Pope—as well as the absence of all willful attachment to sin (even venial—"minor"—sin).

It must also be pointed out that the remission of temporal punishment occurs only after the guilt and eternal punishment of sin have been remitted by adherence to Catholic practice. "The Church grants such indulgences after the guilt of sin and its eternal punishment have been remitted by sacramental absolution or by perfect contrition."[15]

Indulgences and Christ's Atonement

The problem with indulgences is evident from the biblical teaching on the atonement. The necessity for indulgences assumes that the death of Christ did not forgive all divine punishment for sin. We are either eternally forgiven—or we are not forgiven. The Bible teaches that God "forgave us *all* our sins" (Colossians 2:13) and that we *now* have peace with Him (Romans 5:1). Therefore, for the true believer, no punishment whatever is *owed* to God in this life or in the next.

This is not meant to deny the fact that the Bible teaches God may also *discipline* believers. Hebrews 12:6-7 teaches us that "the Lord disciplines those He loves, and He punishes [Greek *mastigoō*—"whips"] everyone He accepts as a son." We can find many examples in the Bible. Although King David's sins against Bathsheba and Uriah were forgiven, he nevertheless had to suffer the discipline of God for what he had done as Nathan the prophet declared.

To sum up, the distinction between the Catholic and the biblical view of divine chastisement of believers includes many critical points. For example, first, chastisements are for believers, but the Catholic Church typically places these on unbelievers (see Hebrews 12:6-7 above). Second, when discipline occurs, the punishment is remedial, not retributive. Third, God is not restricted to using the Catholic Church as the instrument of His discipline; He sovereignly decides how, when, and what means to use. Fourth, biblically, this kind of punishment is done on earth, not in purgatory. Fifth, both biblically and in the experience of Christians, God often does not discipline believers for their sins—otherwise there would be almost no end to His chastisement. Sixth and most important, the punishments for believers' sins cannot be indulgenced by money or any other means, because this defeats the entire purpose of God's loving discipline.

24

WHAT IS THE ROSARY?

The importance of the Rosary is difficult to overestimate.[1] According to Catholic Tradition, it supplies a Catholic with spiritual power and forgiveness of sins—as well as many blessings and graces from God. Pope Paul VI stated in his apostolic exhortation *Marialis Cultus* (February 2, 1974) that the Rosary was the pious practice that to his mind, has correctly been called "the compendium of the entire Gospel."[2]

Pope John Paul II declared October 2002 to October 2003 as "The Year of the Rosary." In his apostolic letter *Rosarium Virginis Mariae* (Rosary of the Virgin Mary), he too declared that the Rosary "has all the depth of the Gospel message in its entirety, of which it can be said to be a compendium....How many graces have I received in [all] these years from the Blessed Virgin through the Rosary."[3]

The Rosary is comprised of both mental prayer and vocal prayer. In mental prayer the participant meditates on the major *mysteries* (particular events) of the life, death, and glories of both Jesus and Mary. The vocal aspect involves the recitation of 15 *decades* (portions) of the "Our Father" and "Hail Mary" prayers, which involve contemplating 15 principal virtues practiced by Jesus and Mary.[4]

The Benefits of the Rosary

The 15-volume *Catholic Encyclopedia* observes of the Rosary that through a "long series of papal utterances it has been commended to the faithful." Further, according to Tradition, St. Dominic (circa 1170–1221) claimed Mary had revealed to him that the Rosary was "an antidote to heresy and sin."[5] Various Popes have emphasized that the Rosary appeases God's anger, makes salvation more easily attainable, and brings the favors of Mary to the Catholic believer, for "Jesus and Mary reward in a marvelous way those who glorify Him."[6]

Consider the following blessings authoritatively pronounced upon recitation of the Rosary:

> [Allegedly said by an apparition of Mary:] When you say your Rosary the angels rejoice, the Blessed Trinity delights in it, my Son finds joy in it too and I myself am happier than you can possibly guess. After the Holy Sacrifice of the Mass, there is nothing in the Church that I love as much as the Rosary....I shall see to their salvation if only they will sing the Rosary, for I love this type of chanting.[7]

> The Rosary recited with meditation on the mysteries brings about the following marvelous results: it gradually gives us a perfect knowledge of Jesus Christ; it purifies our souls, washing away sin; it gives us victory over all our enemies; it supplies us with what is needed to pay all our debts to God and to our fellow men, and finally, it obtains all kinds of graces for us from almighty God.[8]

In a great deal of Catholic literature we are told the Rosary is so powerful that it will certainly help to forgive sins and even save one's soul from hell. In other words, it is also part of the process of maintaining and increasing justification. And it is something certainly believed in by hundreds of millions of Catholics. However, as is true for so many Catholic doctrines, the Bible says not a word about recitation of the Rosary.

25

What Is Purgatory?

In Dostoyevsky's novel *The Brothers Karamazov*, Alyosha, the youngest brother, comments about those in hell, "Even if there were material fire, they would be genuinely glad of it, for I fancy that in material agony the much more terrible spiritual agony would be forgotten, even though for a moment." This comment illustrates the horrifying nature of hell and brings us to a discussion of the doctrine of purgatory.

As with extrabiblical Catholic doctrine in general, the doctrine of purgatory originated in Church Tradition—through, among other things, statements by 1) the allegorist Origen, who believed in the pre-existence of souls and the salvation of Satan; 2) Tertullian, who became a Montanist (a member of a second-century ascetic sect); 3) Augustine; and 4) Gregory I (Pope 590–604), whose stories relating to his visions of the afterlife (see his *Dialogues*) became important for developing the doctrine during the Middle Ages.[1]

Catholic teaching on purgatory was officially proclaimed as dogma in 1438. This means that, until that year—in fact, for more than a millennium—belief in the doctrine was not required. Today, however, it has assumed an immense importance, in that it actually completes the final justification of the Catholic. Despite the hope of some, the Church has not reversed its teaching: "Purgatory is a defined doctrine of the Catholic faith. As a Catholic you must believe in it."[2]

Purgatory is a temporary but torturous hell[3] that almost all Catholics must endure to work off the final punishment for their sins. Only perfect people get to heaven, and the Church agrees there are very few perfect people. Because no one can enter heaven with even the slightest stain of sin, "therefore anyone less than perfect must first be purified before he can be admitted to [heaven]."[4]

Specifically, purgatory cleanses the guilt of sins already forgiven and deals with the sins already confessed but not atoned for. Catholicism believes that penance (see question 22) may be performed not only by good works in this life but also through hellish suffering endured in purgatory after death. As a result, those in purgatory are labeled "the Church Suffering who have died in grace and whose souls are being purged in purgatory."[5] In essence, "the temporal punishments for sins are atoned for in the purifying fire…by the willing bearing of the expiatory punishments imposed by God."[6]

Although technically the souls in purgatory cannot make "true" satisfaction for their sins,[7] remaining in purgatory and enduring punishment for sin is believed to both cleanse individuals of the remnants of sin and permit them entrance into heaven as newly perfected people.[8]

The Catholic Encyclopedia summarizes the teaching:

> The souls of those who have died in the state of grace suffer for a time a purging that prepares them to enter heaven.…The purpose of purgatory is to cleanse one of imperfections, venial sins, and faults, and to remit or do away with the temporal punishment due to mortal sins that have been forgiven in the Sacrament of Penance. It is

an intermediate state in which the departed souls can atone for unforgiven sins before receiving their final reward.…"Purgatorial punishments" may be relieved by the offerings of the living faithful, such as Masses, prayers, alms, and other acts of piety and devotion.[9]

Why Purgatory?

The nature of the Catholic doctrines of salvation and justification requires a doctrine like that of purgatory. If our personal righteousness and the suffering of Christ for our sin are somehow insufficient, then what these lack must be made up by the believer's own increasing righteousness and personal suffering for sin. For Catholics, Christ's righteousness and atonement did not supply all that was necessary for the believer's salvation and entrance into heaven.

Catholics are correct on one point: Only perfect people get into heaven. The issue, then, is how one acquires perfection. Is it on the merits of Christ and His righteousness alone, which are freely credited to the believer by faith—or is it by our own good works, our maintaining of and increasing in justification, and our penitential suffering here and in purgatory?

Biblically, if God has already forgiven all a person's sins and declared a person perfectly righteous through justification, then he or she is already perfect in His sight—100-percent perfect. If one already has the righteousness *of Christ* credited to one's account, nothing is lacking as far as God is concerned because nothing more could possibly be required. The Bible does not teach that purgatorial suffering is necessary in order to enter heaven, because "by one sacrifice he [Jesus] *has made perfect forever those who are being made holy*" (Hebrews 10:14). By faith in Christ alone, first we are made perfect in God's eyes—and then we grow in personal holiness.

Purgatory further has no biblical basis; it is not a mere temporal hell that Jesus told us to fear, but the one that is endless (see Matthew 25:46; Luke 12:5).

Roman Catholicism, Protestantism, and the Virgin Mary

26

Who Is Mary According to Rome?

Significant areas of Catholic doctrine and practice are related to the person and work of Mary, the mother of Jesus. Her unique relationship to God is usually discussed in a trinity of functions: 1) *Co-redemptrix,* 2) *Mediatrix,* and 3) *Queen of Heaven.* As Co-redemptrix, she cooperates with Christ in the work of saving sinners. As Mediatrix of all graces, she now dispenses God's blessings and grace to the spiritually needy. As Queen of Heaven, she rules providentially with Christ the King of Heaven.[1] Although views in Catholicism vary, Mary has usually been elevated above all the prophets, apostles, saints, Popes, and even the Catholic Church itself. In the words of Pope Paul VI, "The place she occupies in the Church [is] 'the highest place and the closest to us after Jesus.'"[2] Vatican II "admonishes all the sons of the Church that the cult, especially the liturgical cult, of the Blessed Virgin, be generously fostered."[3]

The Bible says very little about Mary, yet the Catholic Church has developed an exhaustive systematic and practical theology regarding her. If Mary were who the Church says she is, there would without question be clear scriptural support. Yet there is nothing in

Scripture or in history that indicates Mary was conceived without sin, gave birth to only one child (Jesus), played a vital role in Christ's offering of Himself on the cross and in mankind's salvation, was bodily taken into heaven, now intercedes before Christ on behalf of all mankind, performs miracles for the faithful, can remove Catholics from purgatory, or should actually be prayed to and can forgive sin (the prerogatives of deity alone). Many Catholic theologians will in large part acknowledge the lack of scriptural support, but because Rome declares every one of these things infallibly true, such teachings are accepted as "the Word of God."

Some of the teachings from Catholic Tradition about Mary include the following:

1. *Her immaculate conception.* This doctrine teaches that Mary was born without original sin and was therefore sinless throughout her life. Biblically, however, she deemed herself a sinner—she made a purification offering to the priest and rejoiced in "God my savior" (Luke 1:47; 2:22-24).

2. *Her perpetual virginity.* This dogma asserts that Mary had no children after Jesus. However, the Bible records that Joseph kept her a virgin only "*until* she gave birth to a son" (Matthew 1:25). Jesus clearly had at least seven brothers and sisters. (These were not cousins, as is sometimes claimed. The normal Greek word for "cousin," *anepsios,* is not used in the Bible text, but the word for "brother," *adelphos*—see Matthew 13:55-56.)

3. *Her bodily assumption, or physical ascension, into heaven.* Because of her sinlessness, it is taught, Mary never experienced physical death. Instead she was raised bodily into the presence of Christ the King, where she now functions as "Queen of Heaven," dispensing supernatural graces to all the faithful. No biblical verse makes any mention of this.

4. *Her role as co-redemptrix and mediatrix of all graces*. This doctrine holds that the obedience and sufferings of Mary were essential to secure the full redemption bought by Christ. Again, no Scripture verse even hints at this.

5. *Mary's right to veneration (worship)*. Because of her unparalleled role in the economy of salvation, Mary is worthy of special adoration, which for all practical purposes constitutes worship. There is no suggestion of this anywhere in the Bible.

In our next two questions, we will discuss points 4 and 5.

27

In Her Role as Co-Redemptrix, Does Mary Function as Another Savior?

Mariology is defined as the study of that theology "which treats the life, role and virtues of the Blessed mother of God" and which "demonstrates...her position as Co-Redemptrix and Mediatrix of all graces."[1]

Although the Catholic Church would reject such a designation, for all practical purposes, Mary does function as another savior. She is undeniably godlike—far above the angels—and second in power and authority to only the Trinity. Indeed, in the citations below, Mary's omnipresence (presence everywhere) and omnipotence (all-powerfulness) are more than hinted at—around the world, she hears the prayers of and supernaturally helps the hundreds of millions of Catholics that call upon her. For instance, take the classic Marian prayer:

> O Mother of Perpetual Help,...in thy hands I place my eternal salvation and to thee do I entrust my soul....For, if thou protect me, dear Mother, I fear nothing; not from my sins, because thou wilt obtain for me the pardon of them; nor from the devils, because thou art more powerful than

all hell together; *nor even from Jesus,* my Judge himself, because *by one prayer from thee he will be appeased.* But one thing I fear, that in the hour of temptation I may neglect to call on thee and thus *perish miserably....*[2]

Consider also some recent papal and conciliar pronouncements on Mary:

- Pope Pius XI (1922–1939) said, "With Jesus, Mary *has redeemed the human race.*"[3]

- The conclusion of Pope Pius XII (1939–1958) in his 1943 encyclical *Mystici Corporis* was that Mary herself actually offered Christ on Golgotha: "Who, free from all sin, original or personal, and always most intimately united with her Son, *offered him on Golgotha to the eternal Father...*for all the children of Adam."[4]

- In his *Marialis Cultus* (February 2, 1974), Pope Paul VI (1963–1978) affirmed this:

  This union of the Mother and the Son and the work of redemption reaches climax on calvary, where Christ "offered Himself as the perfect sacrifice to God" (Hebrews 9:14) and where Mary stood by the cross (cf. John 19:25), "suffered grievously with her only-begotten Son. There she united herself with a maternal heart to his sacrifice, and lovingly consented to the immolation of this victim which she herself had brought forth" and so *was offering* to the Eternal Father.[5]

- Vatican II (1962–1965) declared, "Taken up to heaven, she *did not lay aside this saving role,* but by her manifold acts of intercession *continued to win for us gifts of eternal salvation.*" Mary is seen as "used by God not merely in a passive way, but *as cooperating in the work of human salvation* through free faith and obedience."[6]

All this explains the Catholic Church's adoration and worship of Mary. According to Rome, in a very real sense she did win our salvation by the sacrificial, suffering role she played in the birth, life, and death of Christ. And she continues this role through her queenly reign in heaven, where she daily dispenses supernatural grace to some one billion Catholics.

Thus, expressions of devotion to Mary are everywhere. In his encyclical *Redemptor Hominis*, ("redeemer of mankind") Pope John Paul II titled his last chapter "The Mother in Whom We Trust." Some Catholics have even referred to Mary as "the Spouse of the Holy Spirit."[7] In *The Catholic Response,* apologist Dr. Peter Stravinskas remarks that "one cannot ignore this woman, lest one risk distorting the gospel itself."[8]

Co-Redemptrix?

Again, although Mary did not personally die for the sin of the world, by giving birth to the Messiah and by giving Him moral support and other comfort, Mary can be seen as *indirectly* helping to atone for the sin of the world. Of her temporal earthly sufferings, *The Catholic Encyclopedia* teaches that she "endured them *for our salvation.*"[9] Further,

> In the power of the grace of Redemption merited by Christ, Mary, by her spiritual entering into the sacrifice of her Divine Son for men, *made atonement for the sins of men* and…*merited the application of the redemptive grace of Christ.* In this manner she cooperates in the subjective redemption of mankind."[10]

Mediatrix?

Although the Catholic Church maintains that Mary's role does not obscure or diminish the efficacy of Christ as the one Mediator, a good portion of the Church also teaches that Christ could never have *become* the Mediator without Mary. When Mary accepted the angel's announcement that she would bear Jesus, Catholic Tradition holds that her statement, "Be it done unto me according to thy word" (Luke 1:38 DRV) was a command. Thus, if Mary had not "commanded" it, then—at least according to the "maximalist" theological position within the Catholic Church—there would have been no redemption.

The Catholic Catechism discusses Mary's role as one of "Mediatrix Par Excellence," noting her "vicarious assistance" to mankind. In the following citation we see the extent to which Mary is adored as a "savior":

> Mary's title to Mediatrix-in-atonement rests on the pain she freely underwent in union with her Son. The sins of men called for suffering from the God–Man, and he wished his mother to share in the pain as she was the one whom he loved most...*Alongside her Son, Mary has become part of this plan* [of justification] *by contributing her share to the justification of the human race, beginning with herself and extending to everyone ever justified.*"[11]

If the above statements do not describe Mary as a true savior from sin, then words have no meaning. But if she is a true savior, then to that extent Catholicism detracts from the glory due Christ alone—because only He hung on the cross.

28

Is Mary Worshiped in the Roman Catholic Church?

Catholic theology draws a line between the worship offered to God and that offered to Mary. The specific terms used are *latria*—adoration which is due God alone; *dulia*—veneration offered to the saints; and *hyperdulia*—special veneration given only to Mary. This distinction is virtually impossible to maintain in practice. Even Catholic writings often confuse or blur terms such as *veneration, adoration,* and *worship* when referring to God and Mary.[1] There is abundant opportunity for such confusion, since Rome has at least fourteen "feasts of Mary"—special days "set aside to *worship God* with special commemoration of events referring to Mary the mother of God."[2]

For example, when the average Roman Catholic invokes the aid of Mary as a heavenly, all-powerful, all-knowing intercessor, whether on earth or in purgatory, or asks her to beseech Jesus to forgive their sins, it is hard to imagine that in that moment he or she is distinguishing between *latria, dulia,* and *hyperdulia.*

Who Is Actually Deity?

In *The Roman Catholic Church in History,* Dr. Walter Martin outlined what he called the "seven steps to deity" that, in the end, made Mary a god. In the following chart we have summarized and adapted Martin's evaluation:

Mary	Jesus
Mother of God	Son of God
Sinless (Immaculate Conception)	Sinless
Perpetual virgin	Born of a virgin
Ascended (assumed) bodily into heaven	Ascended bodily into heaven
Queen of heaven	King of heaven
Mediatrix of All Graces to Mankind	Dispenser of redeeming grace to all mankind
Co-Redemptrix with Christ in the salvation of mankind	Redeemer and Savior of mankind

The above chart indicates that Mary's person and work is quite parallel to that of Jesus Christ. Though Christ *alone* is worthy of glory to receive our prayer, praise, and worship, Catholics pray to Mary. They ask her to forgive their sin. They expect her to intercede for them with Jesus on their behalf, on earth and in purgatory. Nonetheless, the Catholic Church officially claims that its Mariology does not subtract from the worship and honor due Christ as God and Mediator.[3] But the fine distinctions made by Catholic theologians as to forms of worship "are usually not reflected in the practice of the faithful," according to *The Catholic Encyclopedia.* As it further notes, as far back as "the sixteenth century, as evidenced by the spiritual struggles of the Reformers, the image of Mary had largely eclipsed the centrality of Jesus Christ in the life of believers."[4]

In conclusion, the Marian traditions of Rome detract from the worship that Christ alone is worthy of; they cast a lengthy shadow of doubt upon His sufficiency to intercede for all believers; and they undermine His exclusive saving role.

29

WHO IS MARY ACCORDING TO THE BIBLE?

In spite of Mary's supreme importance in the Catholic Church, there is a complete absence of even the mention of her name in the New Testament epistles. Apart from Acts 14, Mary is mentioned nowhere outside the Gospels. And even in the Gospels, her spiritual power and authority are essentially non-existent. Neither Jesus Christ, nor Paul, nor any other biblical writer ever gave Mary the place or devotion the Catholic Church has given her for a thousand years. And it is crucial we consider that the New Testament letters were written specifically for the spiritual guidance of Christians, and that they have a great deal to say about both doctrine and worship.

Catholic leaders themselves acknowledge that scriptural support for all these traditional doctrines about Mary is lacking. Concerning Mary's assumption into heaven, Keating writes, "Where is the proof from Scripture? Strictly, there is none." Of Mary's role as Mediatrix he comments, "Mary is the Mediatrix of all graces because of her intercession for us in heaven. *True, scriptural proofs for this are lacking.*"[1] Dr. Ludwig Ott, in *Fundamentals of Catholic*

Dogma, notes that "the doctrine of the Immaculate Conception of Mary is not explicitly revealed in Scripture."[2]

What *does* the Bible teach about Mary?

- *The Bible assumes Mary was a sinner like the rest of us.* Why? Because the Scripture emphasizes that all men and women, universally, are sinful (Romans 3:10-32; Psalm 51:5; Galatians 3:22; Romans 3:23; 5:12; and others). Therefore, Mary's prayer beginning in Luke 1:46 that God is her "Savior" rings true. By contrast, there are numerous statements in Scripture declaring that only Christ was perfect and without sin (2 Corinthians 5:21; Hebrews 4:15; 1 Peter 2:22; Hebrews 7:26; and others).

- *Luke 1:28 says simply that Mary was favored by God by being chosen to bear the Messiah.* A profound privilege indeed, but God never says that, as a result, she can now bestow favors and grace upon all mankind.

- *Mary was not a perpetual virgin because she had at least seven other children after Jesus:* "Isn't this the carpenter's son? Isn't his mother's name Mary, and aren't his brothers James, Joseph, Simon and Judas? Aren't all [not both] his sisters with us?" (Matthew 13:55-56). On this point, Catholic apologists can only offer a series of arguments from silence. And there is no justification for assuming Mary's other children were really cousins or more distant relatives—or perhaps even adopted or through another marriage (see also Matthew 12:46; John 2:12; 7:3-5; Acts 1:14; 1 Corinthians 9:5).

- *Apart from her role as bearer and mother of the Messiah, Mary was not unique or especially blessed.* Luke 11:27 records that "one of the women in the crowd raised her voice and said to Him [Jesus], 'Blessed is the womb that bore You and the breasts at which You nursed.' But He said, '*On the contrary,* blessed are those who hear the word of God and observe it'" (NASB). In fact, by Jesus' words, "on the contrary" we see that those who obey God are *more blessed* than if they had given birth to Him.

Jesus acted similarly in Matthew 12:46-50, again denying any special status to Mary. When she wished to see Him, He told the crowd that His true mother, brother, and sister—that is, His true family—was "whoever shall do the will of my Father who is in heaven."

How can the attitude of Jesus Himself be reconciled with Catholic teaching? It cannot. Jesus often referred to Himself as "the Son of Man," but never once, as Catholics do, as "the Son of Mary."

- *Mary cannot be a mediator in any sense between God and man* because "there is...*one* mediator between God and men, the man Christ Jesus" (1 Timothy 2:5-6). In contrast, consider the conclusions of an official publication of the Church: "There is one mediator between Christ and men, the Holy Mother Mary, Mary is the way, the truth and the life. No man comes to Jesus but by Mary."[3]

There is one final consideration before we leave Rome's teaching on Mary. In scores of countries around the world, Marian devotion has become blended with occult phenomena. There are seemingly endless revelations that have come from apparitions and physical materializations of "Mary." These revelations universally support Catholic teachings that are opposed to biblical teachings—on critical subjects like salvation. The most logical explanation for these thousands of supernatural manifestations is that supernatural powers are imitating Mary in order to lead people further away from God. (Having read a good many Marian revelations, we have yet to find one that is in accord with Scripture.)

In conclusion, no Christian can hold to the Bible's teaching on Jesus Christ and also accord to Mary the spiritual privileges and functions granted her by the Catholic Church.

ROMAN CATHOLICISM AND JESUS CHRIST: IS THE ROMAN CATHOLIC VIEW OF THE UNIQUE PERSON AND WORK OF JESUS CHRIST BIBLICAL?

30

ARE THE PERSON AND WORK OF CHRIST COMPROMISED BY CATHOLIC TEACHINGS?

Does the Catholic Church offer the same Jesus Christ to the world as the One found in the New Testament? Most people would probably answer "yes"—however, we have seen how Catholic Tradition has overridden many biblical doctrines, and this is also the case for the crucial doctrine of Jesus Christ.

His Atonement

As to the work of Christ on the cross, Roman Catholic teaching on Mary, indulgences, the sacraments, the Mass, and purgatory all indicate that Christ did not fully and finally atone for all sin. But the Jesus Christ of the Bible *did* atone for all sin. However, Rome's teachings imply that the individual—with the help of, for example, the sacraments—actually makes atonement and satisfaction for his or her own sin. For example: "Through Christ's act of propitiation...[man's] *right to heaven* and the *means* of attainment, namely, *the sacraments,* was made known to the apostles." And as we saw earlier: "The guilt of sin and its eternal punishment have been remitted by sacramental absolution or by perfect contrition"; "[in purgatory] the departed souls can atone for unforgiven sins."[1] Further, "Mary, by her spiritual entering into the sacrifice of her Divine Son for men, *made atonement for the sins of men....*"[2]

Teachings like these indicate the Catholic Church presents "another Jesus" (2 Corinthians 11:4 ɴᴀꜱʙ), who offers merely the possibility of salvation—conditioned upon our good works and obedience to the church. Despite orthodox pronouncements on the doctrine of the Trinity, the Christ of Catholic faith may logically be considered a different Christ. Having orthodox or orthodox-sounding doctrinal statements is no guarantee that the words and concepts used have the same meanings as in the Bible (see question 13). If numerous additional requirements are necessary for sin to finally be forgiven, then Christ's atonement *alone* did not fully or *actually* forgive sin and its penalty.

His Person

A similar situation exists for the doctrine of the Person of Christ. Catholic tradition tends to undermine the unique nature of Christ's Person through its teachings on 1) Mary; 2) the Mass (transubstantiation and the host—see questions 19 and 20); and 3) its view about the continuing or cosmic nature of the incarnation. In regard to the first, the 1994 Catechism tells us, "Catholic *Christology* is unintelligible without knowing the role of Christ's mother in the development of faith from the simple merit of the gospels to the elaborate Mariology of modern times."[3] In regard to the second and third points, just as the Catholic Church continually "re-sacrifices" Christ at the Mass, it also continually incarnates Him in the Church—and in addition, for many mystical Catholics, even in the creation itself.

According to Catholicism, the host *is* God and, as we have seen, is therefore to be worshiped. Keating argues, "What they worship is Christ, and they believe the bread and the wine are turned into his actual Body and Blood, including not only his human nature, but also his divine nature. If Catholics are right about that, then surely the host deserves to be worshipped, since it really is God."[4] "The greatest act of adoration is [the] sacrifice [of Christ] that is most worthily offered in the Mass."[5]

If Christ is actually present in His human nature in the host, it must be conceded that Christ is omnipresent in His human nature every time the host is offered anywhere in the world. Traditional Christology distinguishes between the two natures of Christ—the divine and the human—but it is adamant they cannot be confused. So how is it possible for the human nature of Jesus to be offered in the host unless we accept the assertion that His humanity is omnipresent—thus ascribing to it a contradictory divine attribute? In other words, do we take seriously the biblical limitations of the human nature of Christ?

This illustrates the problem Catholic Christology has with accepting the human nature of Christ, which is why it has often been charged with *docetism*—the view that Christ only *appeared* to be a man. Catholic theologian Tom Beaudoin, a postdoctoral fellow at Boston College notes, "Indeed, one could speak of a tradition of Roman Catholic docetism that has existed in doctrine, theology, spirituality, piety—throughout everyday Catholic life—for 20 centuries."[6]

Christ Incarnate in the Church

There is another area in which Roman Catholic theology distorts the Person of Christ. The uniqueness, authority, and sufficiency of Christ are altered through the teaching that the Catholic Church *itself* includes the real sphere of the incarnation, and is therefore a kind of "second Christ." This does not uplift the Church, but rather brings Christ down to the level and function of Catholic teaching and practice. "According to Catholic teaching, the Church is Jesus Christ 'available' to the point that the Church exists along side of Christ, almost like a second person of Christ....As such it is necessary to salvation."[7]

In the words of Catholic theologian Brom, "The Mother church is so filled with this forever living God–man that it ought to be called a continued Incarnation."[8] The idea of the incarnation as a cosmic principle, or the idea of a progressive incarnation of Christ into His church, is foreign to biblical teaching. Its real consequence is to diminish Christ, His person and work, His glory and honor.

Vatican II described Christ and the Roman Catholic Church not as two realities, but as "one interlocked reality":

> Christ is always present in His Church, especially her liturgical celebrations. He is present in the sacrifice of the Mass, not only in the person of His minister, "the same one now offering, through the ministry of priests, who formerly offered Himself on the cross," but especially under the Eucharistic species. By His power He is present in the sacraments, so that when a man baptizes it is really Christ Himself who baptizes....Christ indeed always associates the Church with Himself....It follows that every liturgical celebration, because it is an action of Christ the priest and of His Body the Church, is a sacred action surpassing all others.[9]

In other words, Jesus Christ Himself is the one performing all the practices that dilute and undermine His own atonement.

This alleged indissoluble unity between Christ and the Catholic Church offers one apparent reason why the Catholic Church considers itself infallible. To listen to the Catholic Church *is* to listen to Christ, for they are one and the same thing—the Catholic Church is His continuing incarnation and expression. Thus, the "living" Word of God as reflected in Roman Catholic Tradition is truly Jesus Christ, who continues to infallibly speak through the teaching office of the Church. For example, even though it was human tradition, and not Christ, that made the act of marriage a Roman Catholic sacrament, according to the Church, "the Sacrament of matrimony...was raised by Christ to the dignity of a sacrament (canon law 1055)."[10] In sum, whatever the Catholic Church does officially, so Christ does. To deny the church is to deny Christ.

But if the decisions of Church Tradition are really the decisions of Jesus Christ, this is tantamount to impugning both the infallibility and holiness of Jesus Christ because on many occasions these decisions have been wrong or immoral.

To conclude, while commonalities do exist between the Catholic and biblical views, the Jesus Christ of the Catholic Church is not the Jesus Christ of the Holy Bible.

Roman Catholicism, Protestantism, and the Pope

31

Was Peter the First Pope?

The Catholic Church believes that Jesus appointed Peter as the first Pope and sent him to Rome to institute the papacy. Let us compare this belief with the Bible.

1. The institution of such a critically important office would inevitably be declared in Scripture, but Scripture is silent about it.

2. The "rock" of Matthew 16:18-19 upon which Jesus would build His church was not Peter himself, but his confession of Christ as the Messiah, as clearly indicated by the context. (Jesus appointed 12 apostles, not one Pope.)

3. Nowhere in the New Testament does Peter exercise the functions of the Pope in regard to authority over all the church or infallibility. Peter never describes himself as a Pope but only as an "apostle" and "fellow elder" (1 Peter 1:1; 5:1).

4. If Peter were the first Catholic Pope, why does he never mention anywhere the importance of doctrines such as the sacraments, Mary, indulgences, penance, purgatory, transubstantiation, or other doctrines uniquely Catholic? To the contrary, he upholds biblical teachings.

5. Though he might have visited Rome, there is no historical proof that Peter was the first bishop of Rome. Further, the apostle Paul spent two full years in Rome in his own quarters and "welcomed all who came to him" (Acts 28:30), yet there is no mention at all of Peter. Is it conceivable that Peter, who had allegedly been in Rome as the Pope for a good length of time, would not even have visited the apostle Paul in his own city—with two full years to do so—especially when he refers to him as "our dear brother Paul" (2 Peter 3:15)?

How can Peter have been the first Pope when no biblical evidence exists to support this?

32

WHAT IS THE DOCTRINE OF PAPAL INFALLIBILITY?

The Catholic Encyclopedia defines the Pope as follows:

The Pope is the Roman Pontiff who, by divine law, has supreme jurisdiction over the universal church (cc. 331–333). He is the supreme superior of all [things] religious (c. 590f.). The Pope may act alone or with a council in defining doctrine for the universal church or in making laws (cf. Infallibility). He is addressed as His Holiness the Pope. By title and right he is: Bishop of Rome, The Vicar of Jesus Christ, Successor of Saint Peter, the Prince of the Apostles, Supreme Pontiff, Patriarch of the West, Primate of Italy, Archbishop and Metropolitan of the Roman province, and Sovereign of the State of Vatican City.[1]

The Catholic Church teaches that, when the Pope speaks *ex cathedra* (that is, "from his chair," or authoritatively, exercising the papal teaching office in a formal public statement), he is infallible, but only in matters of doctrine and morals. The Pope in his person is not infallible, but as a special divine gift, the office of the Pope is infallible. Such infallibility is distinguished from both biblical inspiration and revelation.[2]

> In its Catholic, doctrinal meaning, infallibility is the end result of divine assistance given the Church whereby she is preserved from the possibility and liability to error in teachings on matters of faith and morals. That infallibility was always present in the Church, even from apostolic times.[3]

Further, Catholicism maintains that to deny papal infallibility is to risk loss of salvation[4] and that no Pope or ecumenical council has ever contradicted another:

> *Never* has any Pope officially contradicted what an earlier Pope officially taught about faith or morals. The same may be said about ecumenical councils, which also teach infallibly. No ecumenical council has ever contradicted the teaching of an earlier ecumenical council on faith or morals.[5]

As we will see, this is not true; the Popes and councils have clearly contradicted one another on matters of faith and morals.

True by Definition

Regardless, papal infallibility was not officially defined and promulgated until July 18, 1870, at the first Vatican Council.[6] This was a good 1,800 years after the death of the "first Pope," Peter. Many within the Council protested, and large numbers of other faithful Catholics rejected the doctrine as well, earning for themselves the label "Old Catholics."[7] Within 80 years, some 100,000 of them left Rome over the infallibility decree, even though they were good Catholics in every other respect.

Papal infallibility is sustained solely by papal authority. Thus, the dogmatic constitution *Pastor Aeternus* ("eternal shepherd") asserted that

> it is a dogma divinely revealed: that the Roman Pontiff, when he speaks *ex cathedra,* that is, when in discharge of the office of Pastor and Doctor [Teacher] of all Christians, by virtue of his supreme apostolic authority he defines a doctrine regarding faith or morals to be held by the Universal Church, by the divine assistance promised him in Blessed Peter, is possessed of that infallibility with which the Divine Redeemer willed that his church should be endowed for defining doctrine regarding faith or morals.[8]

"Indeed, given these restrictions, in every comment, and every letter, he is considered infallible."[9] As the Vicar, or official singular representative, of Christ on earth, the Pope has "full, supreme, and universal power over the Church."[10]

While the bishops are also not infallible in themselves, they are such when acting together in agreement with the Pope in an ecumenical council. Vatican II declared "the infallibility promised to the Church resides also in the body of bishops when that body exercises supreme teaching authority with the successor of Peter." As Keating states, "The bishops...also teach infallibly on matters of faith or morals. There have been twenty-one ecumenical councils, and most of them have issued doctrinal or moral decrees. Those decrees are infallible."[11]

All this does not necessarily mean that papal pronouncements that are not *ex cathedra* have no authority. For example, papal encyclicals may be considered divinely authoritative—Catholics are required to accept their doctrinal teachings.

Pius XII stated in *Humani Generis* (1950),

> Nor must it be thought that what is contained in encyclical letters does not of itself demand assent, on the pretext that the Popes do not exercise in them the supreme power [infallibility] of their teaching authority. Rather, such

teachings belong to the ordinary magisterium, of which it is true to say, "He who hears you, hears me" (Luke 10:16).[12]

The Vatican I Decree

The story behind papal infallibility is less well known than the doctrine itself. A thorough discussion of the Vatican I Council can be found in August Bernard Hasler's *How the Pope Became Infallible: Pius IX and the Politics of Persuasion.* Hasler served for five years in the Vatican Secretariat for Christian Unity, where he was given access to the Vatican Archives. There he uncovered crucial documents relating to the council, which had never been studied before. As a result of his research, this learned scholar concluded,

> It is becoming increasingly obvious, in fact, that the dogma of papal infallibility has no basis either in the Bible or the history of the Church during the first millennium. If, however, the First Vatican Council was not free, then neither was it ecumenical. And in that case its decrees have no claim to validity. So the way is clear to revise this Council and, at the same time, to escape from a situation which both history and theology find more and more indefensible. Is this asking too much of the Church? Can it ever admit that a council erred, that in 1870 Vatican I made the wrong decision?[13]

The Council of Trent never decreed papal infallibility. But seven years after Vatican I, Pope Pius IX added words to the decrees of Trent in support of the declaration on papal infallibility. Consider the "Profession of Faith of the Council of Trent." The words in parentheses in the paragraph below were inserted by order of Pope Pius IX in a January 20, 1877 decree.

> I unhesitatingly accept and profess all the doctrines *(especially those concerning the primacy of the Roman Pontiff and his infallible teaching authority)*, handed down, defined and explained by the sacred canons and the ecumenical councils and especially those of this most holy Council of

Trent (*and by the ecumenical Vatican Council*). And at the same time I condemn, reject, and anathematize everything that is contrary to those propositions, and all heresies without exception that have been condemned, rejected, and anathematized by the Church.[14]

As we will now see, the decree of Vatican I has not increased people's trust in the authority of the Church, but has decreased it.

33

IS THE DOCTRINE OF PAPAL INFALLIBILITY CREDIBLE IN LIGHT OF THE TEACHINGS AND DECREES OF CATHOLIC POPES, AND WHAT ARE THE CONSEQUENCES OF THIS DOCTRINE?

If, as Catholics maintain, the Pope speaks "from a tradition of right teaching," that is, Roman Catholicism,[1] then from a biblical perspective the issue of papal infallibility had been long settled by 1870. The Popes cannot possibly be infallible at any point in which they deny Scripture. Thus, every time they teach that salvation is by works, or that baptism or the sacraments are necessary for salvation; every time they teach various unbiblical doctrines about Mary, purgatory, indulgences, and the Rosary, or that the Apocrypha is Scripture, they are teaching error and cannot be considered infallible. Nor can they rightly claim that Christ Himself, incarnate in the Catholic church, has infallibly declared such errors true.

Catholic theologian Hans Küng writes,

> The errors of the Ecclesiastical teaching office in every generation have been numerous and indisputable....And yet the teaching office constantly found it difficult to admit these errors frankly and honestly....For a long time, too, Catholic theologians in their works on apologetics, in the service of the teaching office, were able very successfully to ward off any questioning of infallibility by the use of a

basically simple recipe: either it was not an error, or—
when at last and finally an error could no longer be denied,
reinterpreted, rendered innocuous or belittled—it was not
an infallible decision.[2]

For example, if Pope Liberius (352–366) condemned Athana-
sius, the orthodox defender of Christ's deity, how could he possibly be considered the recipient of divine guidance? Why was
Pope Honorius I (625–638) condemned as a heretic by the Sixth
General Council in 681 and by several subsequent Popes? How
did Pope Sixtus V (1585–1590) produce the error-ridden 1590
edition of the Vulgate? How did Pope Paul V (1605–1621) and
Pope Urban VIII (1623–1644) condemn the true scientific theo-
ries of Galileo?[3]

In addition, Popes have sometimes contradicted one another.
Pope Hadrian II (867–872) declared civil marriages valid, while
Pope Pius VII (1800–1823) declared them invalid. Pope Eugenius
IV (1431–1477) condemned Joan of Arc to be burned as a witch,
while Pope Benedict XV (1914–1922) declared her a saint. Pope
Clement XIV (1769–1774) suppressed the order of the Jesuits on
July 21, 1773; Pope Pius VII (1800–1823) restored them on August
7, 1814.[4]

Küng is only one voice that has pointed out such problems for
years. For example, in *Küng in Conflict,* a compendium of
responses to that theologian with rejoinders, we read that

> Küng, like so many Catholics, was deeply disturbed by
> what he perceived to be a lack of sincerity and truthfulness
> in dealing with changes in doctrines and truth claims. It
> was felt by many to be less than truthful to describe the
> shift from Gregory XVI's solemn condemnation of
> freedom of conscience as "false, absurd madness..." in
> *Mirari Vos* (1832) to Vatican II's declaration on religious
> freedom.[5]

Vatican II is also in conflict with the earlier Catholic doctrine
that salvation outside the Church is not possible.

Popes have even contradicted one another on the recommendation or condemnation of Bible reading.[6] How, then, may Catholics find an infallible guide in the Pope or the teaching office? If they have been wrong in the past, how does anyone know with certainty they are not wrong today?

CATHOLICS, PROTESTANTS, AND THE BIBLE

34

HOW DO CATHOLICS AND PROTESTANTS DIFFER AS TO THE BOOKS (CANON) OF THE BIBLE?

The subject of the biblical canon—those books accepted as Holy Scripture—is one of the most important topics for Christians. It defines the extent of the written Word of God and therefore exposes false claimants to scriptural authority. Jesus, and the Jews, accepted only the 39 books of the Old (Hebrew) Testament as divinely inspired; the early Christians and Protestantism in general add to these the 27 books of the New Testament.

Roman Catholics, however, accept additional writings as Scripture: new portions added to the book of Esther (Additions to the Book of Esther); a new chapter in Daniel (Susanna, or Daniel 13); plus additional books, all of which were written between the Testaments: Tobit, Judith, 1 and 2 Maccabees, Ben Sirach (also called Ecclesiasticus), Baruch, the Letter of Jeremiah, the Prayer of Azariah, and the Wisdom of Solomon.[1] These books are termed *deuterocanonical* ("second canon," or books added to the canon) by Catholics, and *apocryphal* (meaning false, or noncanonical) by Protestants.

In 1546, the Council of Trent officially named and identified the specific apocryphal books it deemed canonical (not all were so deemed), noting, "If anyone does not accept as sacred and canonical the aforesaid books in their entirety and with all their parts,…let him be anathema."[2] For more than a millennium, then, Catholics had not been required to accept these books as Scripture.

Catholics today believe, not that the Council of Trent added these books to the Bible, but rather that the Protestant Reformers "dropped from the Bible books that had been in common use for centuries"—that is, the Apocrypha.[3] In other words, they argue that Protestants actually removed books of Scripture from the canon—books that the Catholic Church had, allegedly, already widely accepted as God's Word at least in principle, if not in official decree.

35

CAN ONE KNOW WITH ASSURANCE THAT THE APOCRYPHA IS NOT SCRIPTURE?

The Apocrypha disqualifies itself from scriptural status. In contrast to the Scriptures, no apocryphal book claims divine inspiration, none were written by a prophet or apostle, and none contain even a single prophetic scripture—2 Maccabees 15:37-38 actually denies inspiration. Not surprisingly, the Apocrypha contains many factual errors. By themselves, Judith and Ecclesiasticus have some two dozen historical or other errors.

Can the Apocrypha be considered God's Word when everyone, Protestant and Catholic, cannot logically deny that it contains demonstrable historical and geographical errors? This destroys the crucial doctrine of divine inspiration, not to mention impugning God's character. To our way of thinking, this single fact alone disqualifies the Apocrypha from canonical status.

Worse, however, the Apocrypha also contains things that are opposed to biblical teaching, such as the idea that good works atone for sin and the doctrines of purgatory, invocation and intercession of the saints, angel worship, the Mass, the creation of the world from pre-existent matter, and others.[1] For example, Ecclesiasticus (also called Wisdom of Jesus Son of Sirach) asserts that "water extinguishes a blazing fire: so almsgiving atones for sin" (3:30).

The numerous factual errors in the Apocrypha have been pointed out in standard works. For example:

> Tobit...contains certain historical and geographical errors such as the assumption that Sennacherib was the son of Shalmaneser (1:15) instead of Sargon II, and that Nineveh was captured by Nebuchadnezzar and Ahasuerus (14:5) instead of by Nabopolassar and Cyaxares....Judith...fits readily into the time of the Maccabean uprising (2nd cent. B.C.), but cannot possibly be historical because of the glaring errors it contains. Thus Nebuchadnezzar was given an impossibly long reign, as was the ruler of Media, while the Assyrians and Babylonians were hopelessly confused and the armies were made to perform impossible feats of mobility....There are also numerous disarrangements and discrepancies in chronological, historical, and numerical matters in the book [of 2 Maccabees], reflecting ignorance or confusion on the part of the epitomist, his sources or both.[2]

Summing up, biblical scholar Dr. René Pache comments,

> Except for certain interesting historical information (especially in 1 Maccabees) and a few beautiful moral thoughts (e.g., Wisdom of Solomon), these books contain absurd legends and platitudes, and historical, geographical and chronological errors, as well as manifestly heretical doctrines; they even recommend immoral acts (Judith 9:10, 13).[3]

Support from Traditions and the Early Church

The councils or statements of Church Tradition are not inerrant, as we have seen, nor are they to be placed in the same category of authority as Scripture. What proves the claim to the Apocrypha's divine inspiration false is the presence of all the errors. In fact, it was the Council of Trent that was "unmindful of evidence, of former Popes and scholars, of the Fathers of the church and the witness of Christ and the apostles" when it made pronouncement.[4]

Pache points out that a key reason for Trent's decision was to respond to the arguments of the Protestant Reformers, who were attempting to defend the principle of *sola scriptura*—that the Bible alone was the final authority for matters of faith and practice, not church tradition. Trent found in the Apocrypha a justification for unbiblical Catholic traditions that were rejected by the Reformers, declaring that

> the Apocryphal books supported such doctrines as prayers for dead (II Macc. 12:44); the expiatory sacrifice (eventually to become the Mass, II Macc. 12:39-46); alms giving with expiatory value, also leading to deliverance from death (Tobit 12:9; 4:10); invocation and intercession of the saints (II Macc. 15:14; Bar. 3:4); the worship of angels (Tobit 12:12); purgatory; and the redemption of souls after death (II Macc. 12:42, 46).[5]

While some in the early church accepted the Apocrypha, others did not. And those who accepted it had different opinions on it. One simply cannot argue that the Apocrypha was accepted implicitly or explicitly by the church as Scripture up until the time of the Protestant Reformation and then thrown out by the Reformers. Rather, it was carefully reasoned arguments, based on full and complete trust in our present 66 books of the Old and New Testaments, that forced the early church to reject the Apocrypha. Former Roman Catholic William Webster points out that John Cosin's book, *A Scholastical History of the Canon,* documents more than 50 major church writers and theologians from the eighth to the sixteenth centuries who held to the view of Jerome (the honored translator of the Latin Vulgate Bible) that the Apocrypha was not Scripture.[6]

The Views of the Jews, of Jesus, and of the Apostles

It is vital to recognize that the apocryphal books were Jewish, compiled before the birth of Christ. Therefore, evaluating the disposition of the Jews regarding their canonicity is paramount:

> Since the New Testament explicitly states that Israel was entrusted with the oracles of God and was the recipient of the covenants and the Law (Rom. 3:2), the Jews should be considered the custodians of the limits of their own canon. And they have always rejected the Apocrypha.[7]

Further, and most important, Jesus and the apostles never accepted the Apocrypha as God's Word. Rather, they "used and believed the groups of books accepted in the Hebrew canon, and none others. For those who find their authority in Christ and His apostles, this would seem to be enough."[8]

Certainly, Jesus and the apostles quoted from the Septuagint—the third-century B.C. Greek translation of the Jewish Scriptures—and some versions of it contain apocryphal books. But this cannot prove the inspiration of the Apocrypha. Further, we have no proof that the Apocrypha was in the version of the Septuagint that Jesus and the apostles used. Assuming it contained these writings, however, the real issue is still what Jesus and the apostles believed about the Apocrypha.

The New Testament never cites the Apocrypha, apart from the possible exception of Jude 14. Neither Jesus nor the apostles ever quoted from it—though they did quote from 35 of the 39 Old Testament books. The Jews, Jesus, and the apostles clearly rejected the Apocrypha as Scripture.

All this helps explain why it required almost 1,600 years for the Catholic Church to officially accept the Apocrypha as Scripture. As a former Catholic, William Webster comments, "I discovered to my surprise that it was the Roman Catholic Church, not the Protestant, which was responsible for the introduction of novel teachings very late in the history of the church."[9] Historically, a book was considered canonical if it was written by a prophet of God, confirmed by an act of God, contained the power of God, told the truth about God, and was accepted by the people of God. The Apocrypha, though, fails on all these counts.

CATHOLICS AND PROTESTANTS TOGETHER?

36

"EVANGELICALS AND CATHOLICS TOGETHER" I AND II— WHAT'S THE BOTTOM LINE?

In the new millennium, there are numerous powerful voices attempting to bring evangelicals and Catholics together as common brethren of a common faith. Apparently, one result is that many thousands of evangelicals now see orthodox Catholics as genuine Christians, despite their beliefs. And many Catholics who call themselves evangelical are now working hard to bring these Christians into the fold of Rome. In his *Pensées,* Blaise Pascal wisely said, "In each action we must look beyond the action at our past, present, and future state, and at others whom it affects, and see the relations of all those things. And then we shall be very cautious."

The Catholic Church has made significant inroads into evangelical faith. Besides much else that could be discussed, we only need consider here the ongoing "Evangelicals and Catholics Together" declarations (to date, in 1994 and 1997, and a 1998 clarification statement.*) The 1994 declaration, which basically concluded that Catholics were true Christians despite their theology, was the impetus for our book *Protestants and Catholics: Do They Now Agree?*†

---

*Appeared in the April 27, 1998 edition of *Christianity Today.*
†Harvest House Publishers, 1995; now out of print.

After the furor caused by ECT I, coauthor Ankerberg, theologian R.C. Sproul, and others met with the evangelical signees in an attempt to address the critical issues involved. While some progress was made at one level, it was unfortunately not enough, because ECT II ("The Gift of Salvation") exhibited the same problem as its sister statement—ambiguity. The 1998 ECT II clarification statement did not resolve the issues, but it did help:

> Our methodology in crafting "The Gift of Salvation" was to study the Bible together and to formulate a statement on salvation derived from and based upon the evidence of Holy Scripture alone. In doing so we were in line with the historic Evangelical insistence on the sufficiency of Scripture and the recent Roman Catholic renaissance in biblical studies.

While there are serious problems with ECT, the motives and goals of the evangelical signees are clearly genuine and, as with Martin Luther and the Reformation, it is always possible that God may finally use these meetings to produce another reformation in the lives of many Catholics. But besides much else, much more work needs to be done with the ambiguity problem before we will know the outcome.

Some of the Results

A great additional problem concerns the authoritative doctrines of Catholicism in themselves and the confusion the two ECT documents are likely to generate among the laity in both camps. Consider two excerpts from ECT II (emphasis added):

> We agree that justification is not earned by *any* good works or merits of our own; it is *entirely* God's gift, conferred through the Father's sheer graciousness, out of the love that he bears us in his Son, who suffered on our behalf and rose from the dead for our justification....We understand that what we here affirm is in *agreement* with what the Reformation traditions have meant by justification by faith alone (sola fide).

As Evangelicals who thank God for the heritage of the reformation and *affirm with conviction* its classic confessions, as Catholics who are conscientiously *faithful* to the teaching of the Catholic Church...we affirm our unity in the gospel that we have here professed. In our coming discussions, we seek no unity other than unity in the truth.[1]

If the Catholic signees now believe the gospel, that's wonderful. The problem is that, through endless doctrinal statements, Rome is opposed to the gospel. So, it is logically impossible for Catholics to "affirm with conviction" historic Reformation principles (which after all rejected Catholicism) and simultaneously be "conscientiously *faithful* to the teaching of the Catholic Church."

The 1997 statement did thankfully admit (as did the 1994 one) that there were many issues requiring "further and urgent exploration," such as

the meaning of baptismal regeneration, the Eucharist, and sacramental grace; *the historic uses of justification as it relates to imputed and transformative righteousness;* the normative status of justification in relation to all Christian doctrine; the assertion that while justification is by faith alone, the faith that receives salvation is never alone; diverse understandings of merit, reward, purgatory, and indulgences; Marian devotion and the assistance of the saints in the life of salvation; the possibility of salvation for those who have not been evangelized.

Clearly, the signees speak only for themselves and not for Rome or evangelical faith. "In fact, the Roman Catholic Church has officially repudiated the definition of a Christian as formulated by...the signers of the ECT documents."[2] As far as Rome is concerned, the three great councils of Trent, Vatican I, and Vatican II remain the basis for determining the boundaries of faith. Below is what these councils have affirmed that a Catholic must believe, upon penalty of being anathematized and suffering the loss of salvation, which can lead to eternal hell:

- that human works cooperate with grace and merit eternal life

- that the Mass is a propitiatory sacrifice for sin

- that the seven Catholic sacraments are necessary for salvation—for example, that water baptism is necessary for salvation and is the instrumental means of regeneration

- that there is no salvation outside the Catholic Church

- that the Pope is infallible

- that the bishops have Christ's authority to rule over the churches on earth and must be submitted to in every area of faith, morals, discipline, and so on

- that confession of sins to a priest, receiving his absolution, and performing acts of penance are the only ways to receive forgiveness of sins after baptism

- that only the Catholic Church has the right to interpret Scripture and that such interpretations are infallible

- that the Apocrypha is Scripture

- that the imputed righteousness of Christ is not the basis for justification, and that justification is not by faith alone

- that in communion the bread and wine are transformed into the literal body and blood of Christ

- that Mary was immaculately conceived and bodily assumed into heaven

- that remedial punishment exists in purgatory[3]

Summing Up

Both ECT statements are not only ambiguous, but also logically contradictory in that they attempt to reconcile inherently opposed worldviews. Because of the ambiguity, the same document can be read in two entirely different ways through the lenses of two exclusive theologies.* The bottom line is, unfortunately, confusion, not clarification.

37

WHY DO SOME PROTESTANTS JOIN ROME?

There are many reasons why a given church member might convert to the Roman Catholic faith. Among these reasons are

- frustration with the barrenness of secular philosophies and the desire to find spiritual reality after living with a spiritually dead church

- an attraction to the formal, high style of worship offered in Catholicism—that is, a response to the emotion generated by Catholic liturgy

- exposure to liberal Protestantism and a resulting confusion over biblical authority and teaching

- the corollary belief to the above—that one must have an authoritative head (Pope) or leader (teaching office) in order to properly interpret the Bible (in other words, the need for an infallible external authority to counteract the alleged theological "uncertainty" of Protestantism and its "private interpretation" of Scripture)

- the desire for Christian "unity," regardless of the cost doctrinally

- simple ignorance—for example, the belief that Jesus Himself might actually have instituted the papal office under the headship of Peter, and that therefore only the Roman Catholic Church could be the one true church

---

* For further discussion of this point, see appendix A.

In fact, there are dozens more reasons why any given individual might join the Catholic Church. And today, no one can deny that among such individuals are some former professed evangelical Christians.

Many stories of conversions to Catholicism are recounted in books on the subject, including *Spiritual Journeys: Toward the Fullness of Faith*. In this book, 27 people tell of their personal pilgrimage to Catholicism. (In appendix B, we look at three individuals in particular who are more well-known among evangelicals: Thomas Howard, Paul Vitz, and Peter Kreeft; afterward, we will examine the reasons given by Scott Hahn, who widely proselytizes for Catholicism by critiquing Protestant faith.)

A Central Problem

Briefly, Howard, Vitz, and Kreeft have all had strong contacts with evangelicalism, appreciate it greatly—and if they were personally associated with it before, they continue to miss aspects of it that they see as tremendous strengths.[1] What is most relevant to us is Kreeft's confession that Catholics really don't understand the biblical gospel at all. Consider the following crucial admission, one consistent with Kreeft's quarter-century-long experience within the Catholic Church:

> At Heaven's gate our entrance ticket, according to Scripture and Church dogma, is not [solely] our good works or our sincerity, but our faith, which glues us to Jesus. He saves us; we do not save ourselves. But I find, incredibly, that 9 out of 10 Catholics do not know this, the absolutely central, core, essential dogma of Christianity. *Protestants are right:* most Catholics do, in fact, believe a whole other religion. Well over 90 percent of students I have polled who have 12 years of catechism classes, even Catholic high schools, say they expect to go to Heaven because they tried, or did their best, or had compassionate feelings to everyone, or were sincere. *They hardly ever mention Jesus.*

Asked why they hope to be saved, they mention almost every-
thing except the Savior.[2]

It would seem this would place Kreeft—and other former evangelicals like him—in a quandary. If the Catholic Church really is the one true Church God has established, and if the Pope is the vicar of Christ on earth, then how did the basic gospel of salvation ever get so perfectly lost in the first place?

Although Kreeft has been "happy as a Catholic for 26 years now" and says, "I am happy as a child to follow Christ's vicar on earth everywhere he leads. What he loves, I love; what he leaves, I leave; where he leads, I follow,"[3] the central predicament of Scripture verses Tradition remains. How can you follow someone who denies what the Bible teaches about such an important issue as salvation?

In light of the above, what do former evangelicals who are now Catholics do with their allegiance to biblical teaching? Kreeft admits that the "serious concern for truth" that he was raised with as a young evangelical is something that "to this day I find sadly missing in many Catholic circles."[4]

This, then, is the issue—the importance of "a serious concern for truth." People may indeed convert to Catholicism for an almost endless number of reasons. But there is one reason that no one ever gives for joining the Catholic Church: conviction regarding biblical authority. No one has ever converted to Catholicism who has consistently and logically maintained an allegiance to the Bible as their sole authority. If the Bible is one's authority, it is impossible to convert to Catholicism.

People therefore have joined Catholicism either because they don't understand the issues involved (they are uninformed or confused), or because they are really not committed to biblical inerrancy and authority, or because they simply prefer what the Roman Church has to offer irrespective of what Scripture teaches. Some will indeed claim that they "met Jesus and are propelled to the Roman Church in obedience to Him."[5] In His own teachings, though, Jesus rejected most of the major doctrines of the Catholic Church, so how could He impel anyone to convert to Catholicism?

To sum up the matter, unless the evangelical church is prepared to accept more and more of its members converting to Roman Catholicism for no solid reason, it should take the education of its members more seriously when it comes to biblical authority, apologetics, and the basic doctrines of the faith.

The Nature of a Christian Church

38

What Makes a Religion Christian?

A leading American evangelical apologetics ministry—one that specializes in the analysis of comparative religion and cult theology—sent out the following standard reply in answer to the question "Is Roman Catholicism biblical?"[1]

1. Does the Catholic Church teach orthodox Christianity? *Answer: Yes.*

2. Does the Catholic Church teach salvation by good works or by faith? *Answer: They teach it by faith.*

3. Does the Catholic Church teach another gospel? *Answer: No.*

Hypothetically, if other Christian ministries who specialize in spiritual discernment would agree with this assessment, then are there truly differences between evangelicalism and Roman Catholicism?

Let's consider the following primary definitions of the term *Christian:*

- *Oxford Dictionary and Thesaurus:* "1. Of Christ's teachings or religion. 2. Believing in or following the religion based on the teachings of Jesus Christ."

- *Macmillan Dictionary for Students:* "1. One who believes in and follows the teachings of Jesus; member of the religion based on those teachings."

The Catholic Church accepts the teachings of Jesus in many respects, but not in the most critical areas—those relating to subjects like divine revelation and authority, the gospel, justification, the atonement, and the afterlife.

Merely having some degree of doctrinal orthodoxy does not prove a religion is Christian. For example, in church history certain unorthodox or heretical sects have accepted the doctrine of the Trinity and yet denied other cardinal doctrines of the faith. Today, Jehovah's Witnesses believe in the inerrancy of the Bible far more consistently than Catholics. Yet no one argues they are Christian except themselves. Mormonism provisionally accepts the Bible as the Word of God and in certain ways believes in the atonement of Christ. Yet few religions are more anti-Christian.[2] Even Muslims are devout monotheists and have various moral views in harmony with the Bible. But none of these religions can properly be classified as Christian because what makes a religion Christian is both 1) a fundamental body of correct (scriptural) doctrinal belief that true Christians have always believed without compromise, and 2) religious practices and a lifestyle among its members that conform to biblical standards.

In sum, the Roman Catholic Church cannot be properly classified as "Christian" because it has

- a different Jesus Christ and a different Mary, resulting in a different doctrine of the Trinity

- a different gospel, resulting in a different doctrine of salvation

- a different Bible and ultimate source of authority, resulting in a different divine revelation

- a different church, resulting in a different witness of Christian faith to the world

- a different afterlife, resulting in a personal fear of death and torture in purgatory, despite Christ's atonement for all sin

- a different sanctification, resulting in increased guilt and defeat in the Christian life, rather than freedom from sin

In the end, Roman Catholicism offers a different God than the God of Jesus Christ, resulting in a different religion than that of biblical Christianity.

Judging by Catholic Standards

Though the Catholic Church has officially defined the identifying marks of what it means to be Christian, it fails to meet its own qualifications. In *The Catholic Encyclopedia* we are told there are four criteria identifying the true Christian church that are endorsed by the Council of Trent, whose decrees remain authoritative for today: 1) oneness of doctrine, 2) the generation of true personal holiness dispensed through the Church's means of sanctification (for example the sacraments), 3) catholicity—that is, universality of mission, and 4) apostolicity—teachings and practices derived from Christ and the apostles.[3]

On the first test, can it logically be maintained that the Catholic Church, as a whole, has a *oneness of doctrine?* In regard to doctrine, the term *catholicity* was classically defined in the fifth-century "Vincentian Canon" as "what has been believed everywhere, always, by all."[4]

Individual Catholics aside, have the Popes and magisterium always maintained unity of doctrine? How is this possible, given the doctrinal contradictions and controversies throughout Catholic history and Tradition, and in the Apocrypha? What about the serious differences found in the various competing forms of modern Roman Catholicism, such as the liberal, moderate, conservative, mystical, and charismatic branches? Does Vatican II agree entirely with Trent? No. Would Trent have agreed with the Vatican I decision to make the Pope infallible? No. What about the "Old Catholic Church," whose members are traditionally Catholic except for denying papal infallibility? Even in the most historically conservative branch, traditional Roman Catholicism, there is no absolute unity of doctrine, as we have seen.

As to the second test, on what biblical basis can *true holiness be said to be dispensed through the Roman Catholic Church* and its beliefs and practices? Biblically, it is clear that sanctification, or growth in holiness, comes principally through the work of the Holy Spirit applied individually to true believers in Christ through the renewing power of both learning Scripture and obeying it. If so, of what value are the Roman Catholic sacraments and other practices for the process of sanctification?

Biblically, if individual Catholics are attempting to earn their own salvation by good works, are they even saved? Roman Catholicism inhibits true sanctification because sanctification is not possible without spiritual rebirth or regeneration (see John 6:63; Colossians 2:23) and the power of the Holy Spirit. Millions of Catholics today think they are Christians when, in fact, they are just Catholics. Of course, the same may be said of many Protestants who, for whatever reason, have personally rejected the gospel. Regardless, the numerous ethical problems in Catholic history and today suggest that holiness has not exactly been dispensed in the manner claimed.

The third Catholic test for identifying the one true Church is *catholicity,* or *universality of mission.* This is a more difficult test to pass than the first two. But do Roman Catholics really have unity of mission? Aren't there competing factions within the Church, each having their own agenda, definition, and outworking of "mission"? In question 2, we mentioned various groupings within modern Roman Catholicism—from nominal to syncretistic, from ethnic to liberal, from mystical and traditional to charismatic and evangelical. Can it logically be argued that all these groupings constitute a "unity of mission"? What of the various sects within Catholicism that don't accept the current Pope?

The fourth Catholic test for identifying the one true Church is *apostolicity,* or agreement with the teachings of Jesus and the apostles. But if the Roman Catholic Church rejects the teachings of Jesus and the apostles, as we have shown earlier, how can it logically be considered "apostolic"?

In sum, the Roman Catholic Church fails all four of its own criteria for authenticity as the one true Christian Church. If Roman Catholicism denies critical biblical doctrine and is not the one true Christian Church according to its own standards, it should not be classified as a Christian religion.

Our discussion to this point underscores a simple fact. Claims to being "Christian" need to be thoroughly evaluated with proper attention to 1) word meanings, 2) doctrine as a whole, and 3) lifestyle and practices.

The Ultimate Question

The issue is not how close a given religion can come to the historic doctrines of Christianity. The issue is whether one accepts the true gospel or not—because if one doesn't, all the rest is irrelevant. Brought down to the personal level, the idea of going to hell forever because you missed the gospel but were 99 percent correct on other doctrines offers small comfort.

That Catholicism accepts many Christian doctrines is irrelevant. That it teaches salvation by works proves it is not a Christian religion. That some people are saved within the Roman Catholic Church only means that some individuals, like Martin Luther, have found salvation by God's grace because they studied the Bible—or because Christians witnessed to them and they were saved by hearing the gospel.

Luther said this: "If I declare with the loudest voice and clearest exposition every portion of God's Truth except for that one little bit which the world and the devil are at the moment attacking, I am not confessing Christ no matter how boldly I may be professing Christ." The gospel—anything but minuscule—is what the world, the flesh, and the devil have always attacked. And it continues to be attacked today—within the Catholic Church.

Therefore, Christians who think Roman Catholicism is truly Christian, "evangelical Catholics" who seek to bring their "separated brethren" back to Rome, and evangelicals who have converted to Rome need to ask themselves where their commitment is to the *gospel*—the doctrine of salvation by grace alone that the world and the devil are at this moment attacking. And if their commitment isn't to an uncompromising stand in defense of that gospel, how can their commitment be to Christ and His church?

A Personal Word to Catholics—
and Many Protestants

We have written this book because we believe there is one vital issue that all Catholics (and many Protestants) need to think through. It is the issue of one's personal salvation.

As a Catholic, you, more than anyone else, are aware that it is not possible in this life to have assurance of salvation—except perhaps in very rare circumstances. Catholic literature emphasizes that a belief in the assurance of salvation is a "presumption upon the mercy of God." It also tells us that mortal sin results in "eternal separation from God" and requires penance for restoration. It emphasizes the personal hazards of so-called *triumphalism*, which is said to be something that "arises out of" an "assurance of having been saved," which is "a dangerous position" to hold.[1]

Because Catholicism teaches that Christians may lose their salvation, "not even faith...or conversion...or reception of baptism...or constancy throughout life...can gain for one the right to salvation." All these are held to be only "the forerunners of attainment" of salvation.[2]

There *Is* Good News

The really good news is that such teaching is not biblical. Jesus Himself taught that faith does bring the right to salvation: "As many as received Him, to them He gave *the right* to become children of God" (John 1:12 NASB).

In addition, the Bible clearly teaches that by faith alone people can know that they are eternally saved; that at the moment of saving faith, a person possesses eternal life. As Jesus taught, "Truly, truly, I say to you, he who believes *has eternal life*" (John 6:47 NASB). And as the apostle John declared, "These things I have written to you who believe in the name of the Son of God, so that you may *know* that you *have* eternal life" (1 John 5:13 NASB).

The Roman Catholic Church does not have the right to tell people that they *cannot* have an assurance of salvation when God clearly says they *can*. In fact, any person on earth—no matter how serious their sins, no matter what religion he or she has been in, from secularism to satanism—at the moment they truly believe in Jesus Christ as their Savior from sin, can know that 1) all their sins are forgiven—past, present, and future; 2) they are fully and completely justified (declared righteous) by God; and 3) they now have an eternal salvation that can never be lost under any circumstances (Romans 8:38-39). This is why the Bible declares,

> Praise be to the God and Father of our Lord Jesus Christ! In his great mercy he has given us new birth into a living hope through the resurrection of Jesus Christ from the dead, and into an inheritance that can never perish, spoil or fade—kept in heaven for you, who through faith are shielded by God's power (1 Peter 1:3-5).

And,

> Those God foreknew he also predestined to be conformed to the likeness of his Son, that he might be the firstborn among many brothers. And those he predestined, he also called; those he called, he also justified; those he justified, he also glorified.
>
> What, then, shall we say in response to this? If God is for us, who can be against us? He who did not spare his own Son, but gave him up for us all—how will he not also, along with him, graciously give us all things? Who will bring any charge against those whom God has chosen?...Who shall separate us from the love of Christ?...

For I am convinced that neither death nor life, neither angels nor demons, neither the present nor the future, nor any powers, neither height nor depth, nor anything else in all creation, will be able to separate us from the love of God that is in Christ Jesus our Lord (Romans 8:29-33,35, 38-39).

Certainly the above listing of things that cannot separate us from God's love would include such items as mortal sins, or lack of penance or confession to a priest. Thus, the biblical truth—the good news for all people—is that they *can* know that they now have eternal salvation.

If you are a Catholic and desire to receive Jesus Christ as your personal Lord and Savior, we urge you to say the following prayer:

> *Dear God, it is my desire to enter into a personal relationship with You on the basis of the death of Your Son, Jesus, on the cross. Although I have believed many things about Jesus, I confess I have never truly received Him individually as my personal Savior and Lord. I have never understood that the Bible teaches that salvation is a free gift You offer me without cost and good works on my part.*
>
> *I now receive Your gift of salvation and Your pardon of my sins, as I fully believe that Christ died on the cross for my sins—all of them. I believe He rose from the dead.*
>
> *It is my desire, Lord Jesus, that You now become my Lord and Savior. I now invite You into my life. I make You the Lord over all areas of my life, including all personal beliefs or practices that are not biblical—not to get saved, but because I love You and want to serve You for saving me.*
>
> *Help me to be committed to studying Your Word and growing as a Christian in ways that honor You. Give me the strength to face difficulty or rejection when it comes to making a stand for You. If it be Your will, and necessary, for me to leave the Roman Catholic Church, give me the strength to do this, and guide me into a good church and fellowship so that I might know and glorify You the more.*
>
> *In Jesus' name I pray this, trusting in Your guidance. Amen.*

APPENDIX A

Further Discussion of the "Evangelicals and Catholics Together" Declarations

Consider the important conclusions of noted Protestant theologian and apologist R.C. Sproul in regard to the ECT declarations:

> Many professing evangelicals have lauded this new initiative as a remarkable achievement that at long last resolves the historical antithesis between Roman Catholics and evangelicals so that the two groups can now see themselves as enjoying a unity of faith in the Gospel....If the issue of justification boils down to two mutually exclusive options, a righteousness in us or a righteousness apart from us, how can the discussion be reconciled? We meet here a clear antithesis that seems incapable of being synthesized by some mutually agreeable compromise. To ameliorate the difficulty, I can think of three possible ways to resolve the dispute: (1) evangelicals can abandon their view of *sola fide* and its foundation upon imputation; (2) Roman Catholics can abandon their view of inherent righteousness; or (3) a formula can be drawn up that is a studied ambiguity by which agreement is reached in words but not in substance, leaving each side the opportunity to maintain its original position.

> Which of these options, if any, was pursued by the signatories of ECT I and II? On the surface it appears that it was #3. That both ECT I and ECT II are ambiguous at

critical points should be clear to anyone who carefully reads the document....That ECT I has conscious ambiguity is without doubt. In a letter circulated to the signatories of ECT I written by Richard John Neuhaus, the chief Roman Catholic architect of the document, he asks the question, "Do we mean the same thing by the words used?" He answers his own question with the emphatic words: "of course not." On at least three occasions the chief evangelical architect, Charles Colson, declared that "after all, we don't mean the same thing by what we said." In response to this disclaimer, I asked Mr. Colson, "If you knew you didn't mean the same thing by the words you used, how can you claim to the world that you have an agreement?"

Dr. Sproul proceeds to discuss some of the problems with the ECT II documents:

I am convinced that these [evangelical] men, both in their [1998] clarification statement and in their formulation of "The Gift of Salvation" [1997] intended to proclaim the historic evangelical position....Although many have claimed that salvation by faith alone was affirmed in this document, unfortunately this was not so. The right words were there, but not the right meanings.

To Charles Colson's credit, it was reported that during the discussions leading up to the final draft of "The Gift of Salvation," he steadfastly insisted that unless *sola fide* was included in the agreement he would not sign it. Colson is convinced that *sola fide* is affirmed and has declared that he could not see how imputation could have been made any more clear than it is in the document....Since imputation goes to the heart of the historic controversy we would have hoped that any attempt to resolve that controversy would have addressed it explicitly and without ambiguity....If we are justified solely on the grounds of the imputed righteousness of Christ, that justification can be neither augmented nor diminished. I need no more purity to be declared righteous by God than the perfect purity of Christ, which requires no more purging of impurity in purgatory....As long as purgatory remains on the table, there is no unity in "the basic dimension" of the Gospel.

Finally, Dr. Sproul hits the nail on the head by showing why orthodox Catholics could sign the document in good conscience, but mean something entirely different than the evangelical signers:

> Rome has always had her version of "forensic" justification. That is, Rome recognizes that justification involves God's legal declaration that the believer is just. This is said to be via the righteousness of Christ. But it is the infused righteousness of Christ with which the believer cooperates and to which the believer assents in order to become inherently righteous. But, Rome teaches, God does not, and will not, declare the believer just until or unless that believer becomes inherently just; hence the need for purgatory. Roman Catholic theology emphatically repudiated Luther's *simul justus et peccator* (the reality that the Christian is simultaneously justified and yet still intrinsically sinful), calling it a legal fiction. Rome repudiates the Reformation concept of forensic justification.
>
> A public manifesto that declares a generic unity of faith and mission and a unity of the Gospel between Roman Catholics and evangelicals...at best confuses the faithful and at worst confuses the Gospel....In conclusion, I see nothing in "The Gift of Salvation" that an orthodox Roman Catholic could not in good conscience sign. The document is flawed by its ambiguity at crucial points. These points must be addressed before there can be any significant resolution of the historic conflict.[1]

What Reasons Do Evangelicals Give for Converting to Roman Catholicism?

Why did Thomas Howard, Paul Vitz, and Peter Kreeft convert to Roman Catholicism? Let's find out.

Thomas Howard

Howard observes, "My recent conversion to Roman Catholicism has puzzled and troubled most of the Evangelicals who know me."[1] Howard left evangelicalism for several reasons. First, he already believed in the authority of Church tradition and increasingly desired a centralized teaching authority. Second, he was troubled by the lack of pastoral accountability that seemed evident in many Protestant churches. Third, he also came to believe in the efficacy of the Catholic sacraments.[2] For example,

> There are so many hundreds of very small Evangelical denominations and congregations. Some of the "cardinal" parishes in Evangelicalism are totally independent: the minister is accountable to no bishop or synod or superior of any description. This tendency began to trouble me, as the years went by....If the Church is anything at all other than a mere clutter. It is apostolic. There has got to be a Magisterium [authoritative teaching office], and not just a clamor of voices. Christianity is not analogous to Islam— a religion of the Book alone....[In the early fathers] we find indeed one holy, catholic, and apostolic Church, and

not a clutter of privately launched enterprises, no matter how earnest or laudable those enterprises might be....

It is the old question of catholicity and apostolicity. What is the Church? Where is the Church? Also, it entails the question of teaching authority. All the heresiarchs believed in the inspiration of the Bible. But who has the warrant to teach the Scriptures? Anyone? Everyone? If we consult the early Church, we find that it was the bishops in council who said to the faithful, "This is the apostolic faith. That which you hear being taught over there is heresy." Christ never doomed his Church to a perennial, *ad hoc* caucus of the whole, with all matters of morals and dogma forever on the table, forever up for grabs. But alas, this turns out to be the case where there is no Magisterium.

I eventually found myself crowded along to the place where I either had to say, "But none of this matters: all God wants is for us to be earnest and fervent," or I had to say, "Hum. Independence won't do. That is not the apostolic pattern." Who am I to disassociate myself from this 2000-year-old train of apostles, fathers, bishops, martyrs, confessors, doctors, widows, virgins, and infants, who testify to what Christ's Church is?[3]

Questions for Thomas Howard

In response to the above, we might ask the following. First, does the lack of pastoral accountability in *some* churches require the conclusion that Protestantism as a whole maintains no legitimate mechanisms of accountability? We don't think so; the great majority of Protestant churches we have encountered in 35 years are responsible, accountable ones.

Second, we grant that no Christian would deny that, if the church should be anything, it should be apostolic. The apostles were inspired to record the very words of God Himself, and the teachings they gave for Christian belief and living are our standard. But from this fact, does it necessarily follow that the *post*apostolic fathers got their doctrine right in all particulars (they didn't)—or that early and later church tradition has equal weight with Scripture? (It doesn't.) In earlier pages, we have already seen the tragedy of granting church tradition equal authority with Scripture.

Third, we don't think that the phrase "a clutter of privately launched enterprises" does justice to the Protestant tradition, especially when it is implied that matters of morals and dogma are "forever on the table." The thousands of Christian churches that accept the inerrancy of Scripture do, in fact, have an infallible authority for determining correct doctrine and morality—Scripture itself. This means that, even though these churches reject the Catholic magisterium, their morals and doctrines are hardly "forever up for grabs." Biblical doctrine and morality are clearly laid out in Scripture—and all genuine Christian churches that accept biblical authority have found general agreement on these issues without the assistance of the Catholic Church.

Fourth, why should anyone present themselves with a false dilemma claiming that either we must 1) entirely disregard apostolic and postapostolic teaching or 2) convert to Roman Catholicism? Isn't the wiser course to accept the Word of God alone as the authority, then to grant that the early church fathers, being fallible men, wrote both truth and error, and therefore to evaluate their teachings and church tradition as a whole in light of God's Word? Certainly, the *apostles* never taught the doctrines unique to Roman Catholic theology, whether or not some in church history have. Apostolicity belongs to conservative Protestantism, not Catholicism.

All in all, we don't think that the specific reasons Thomas Howard supplies for converting to Catholicism really justify his decision biblically, however sincere it may have been.

Paul Vitz

Former atheistic psychologist Paul C. Vitz became a Catholic because his allegiance to secularism had resulted in an irresolvable "crisis of faith." The truth of Vitz's evaluation is something any fair-minded academic would have to concede today, given the influence of multiculturalism, what is called "political correctness," and other modern-day campus phenomena:

> In particular, the university, the community of scholars, showed itself so without standards, so without the courage of convictions, as to be a kind of joke. The last vestiges of my respect for academia collapsed as I watched the university leadership cave in to various social and political pressures. By the end of the 60's and the start of the 70's my secular ideals were in shreds.
>
> One of my concerns was my deepening disillusionment with the field of [experimental and cognitive] psychology itself.
>
> Even more disturbing was my growing understanding of how other parts of psychology, for example, personality theory and counseling practice, had contributed to the secular madness of what was going on...Modernism in its *essential* nature is subjective, arbitrary and nihilistic.[4]

But in addition, Dr. Vitz's Episcopal Church was very liberal—and apparently provided him with little or no spiritual sustenance:

> Meanwhile, as my understanding of Christian theology deepened, I quickly came into conflict with liberal Christian theology, most of which was Protestant in origin. It was obvious to me that liberal theology was at best a compromise with anti-Christian modernist thought, and at worst a thinly disguised denial of Christ....Unfortunately, the Episcopal Church was dominated by liberal thought, indeed so dominated by it that many couldn't even see it. As far as they were concerned, liberal theology was the only possible way of understanding things. It was then that I first experienced the rigid, narrow-minded character of liberal thought and of so many liberals. I still remember the remark made to me by a young Episcopal priest—his voice dripping with condescension—"You mean you believe in the *bodily* resurrection of Christ?"[5]

One can only have sympathy for those in Dr. Vitz's position: Like modernism, liberal theology is nothing if it is not a road to Hell, both here and in the afterlife. Unfortunately, Dr. Vitz also encountered a series of dramatic visions and various aesthetic or psychological bonds to Catholicism itself. For example:

> These dramatic, unexpected experiences were really something like visions....Along with prayer, reading, and Catholic friends—especially many wonderful priests— these experiences solidified my commitment to the Catholic faith. [Finally,] one of the great liberations in becoming a Catholic was to be part of the universal character of the Church....I sensed a new kinship with people in countries as diverse as Argentina, Poland, and Zanzibar....I was linked to millions of people of all nations, races and cultures.[6]

Our Response to Paul Vitz

Again, we can certainly sympathize with Vitz's frustration with the traps of secularism, the tragedy of his experience under liberal theology—endlessly repeated today—and the dramatic nature of his personal visions. But we would ask whether or not any of these logically justify conversion to Catholicism—if indeed it is not a religion upholding biblical truth. If Scripture is the authoritative standard—and Roman Catholicism, overall, denies what Scripture teaches in key areas—then the Roman Catholic Church cannot be the one true church. So we hope that neither frustrating experiences in the past nor dramatic encounters in the present will cause anyone to neglect adhering to the truth of God's Word. If by chance we have failed to become a member of God's true church, then what is the value of our spiritual fellowship before God?

Peter Kreeft

Kreeft converted to Roman Catholicism because of his rather rigid Calvinist and anti-Catholic background—which allegedly contained many "sincere mistakes" concerning Catholicism. In the end, this apparently rubbed him the wrong way. As well as the need for visible objects (that is, images) to help him love and worship God, he also had several unanswered questions: "Why don't Protestants pray to saints?" "Was only Calvinism correct among all branches of Christendom?" "How could God leave the rest of the world in error?" The result? "Since no good answer seemed forthcoming, I then came to the explosive conclusion that the truth about God was more mysterious—more wonderfully and uncomfortably mysterious—than anything any of us could fully comprehend."[7]

Other reasons for conversion to Catholicism included "a strong intellectual and aesthetic love for things medieval" and the influence of reading the Catholic mystics. He found that the "richness and mystery of Catholicism fascinated me."[8]

However, the central reason for his conversion was the Church's claim to be the only true Church: "There were many strands in the rope that hauled me aboard the ark, though this one—the Church's claim to be the one [true] Church historically founded by Christ—was the central and deciding one."[9]

Again, our only response can be, "If the Roman Catholic Church were indeed the one true church, it could not possibly deny and oppose what the Bible plainly teaches about the critical area of salvation."

Scott Hahn

One final illustration should reveal the seriousness of this issue. Yet another story of conversion to Rome is found in the person of Scott Hahn, author of *Rome, Sweet Home*. In a lecture to a parish in Riverside, California,[10] he begins by claiming that few people really understand what the Roman Church actually teaches—they only know falsehoods they have adopted from erroneous sources. Thus, evangelicals "simply don't understand" Roman Catholicism, "they [only] think they do." This, unfortunately, is the standard response of those who identify themselves as "evangelical Catholics"—no one really understands Catholicism except a Roman Catholic.

Hahn grew up in a nominal Protestant family with little if any church attendance. Later in high school he allegedly accepted Christ as his personal Lord and Savior through the ministry of the Young Life organization.

But as a result of his own spiritual journey and study, Hahn so thoroughly rejected his evangelical upbringing that he now does his best to confirm Roman Catholics in their own beliefs and to convert evangelicals to Catholicism.

Hahn calls the standard evangelical gospel view of salvation—accepting Jesus Christ as one's personal Lord and Savior from sin—"inadequate from a Catholic perspective." He told his listeners, "If you're ever asked by a Protestant, 'Are you born again?' you should say, 'Of course I am. What do you mean by it?' 'Have you accepted Jesus Christ as your personal Lord and Savior?' You should say, 'Yes, of course I have....But that's not *why* I was born again. I was born again because I was baptized.' "

Hahn makes it clear that, for him, evangelicals have only "partial truths and insights" and need Rome to correct their errors on salvation and other important matters.

How did Scott Hahn become a Catholic? In many cases like this we suspect that the real reasons are mostly hidden and the public story may portray only a small part of them. Regardless, Hahn did have a lot of Catholic friends. After he was saved he dated a Catholic girl "very seriously." His best friends in high school were all Catholic. After graduation from high school he went to evangelical Gordon–Conwell Seminary, where he received his M.Div. degree in 1982. This is where he refined his then anti-Catholic views, at least initially, but also where he began his conversion to Catholicism. In his second year at the seminary, his wife did a study on birth control for one of her seminary classes. She concluded it was immoral, bringing her and eventually her husband to agreement with the Catholic Church.

At the same time a professor at Westminster Seminary whom Hahn was thinking of studying with was being expelled for rejecting the doctrine of salvation by grace alone through faith in

Christ alone. Hahn landed smack in the middle of this debate and concluded that the professor, Shepherd, was correct and that therefore Luther was wrong—and that salvation was by both faith and works. This began a very traumatic period of re-evaluation.

After graduation he took a job as a pastor and taught a seminary class at night. He began intensive studies into the issues separating Catholicism and evangelicalism. In his studies of both Old and New Testaments he kept "seeing" that what Catholic scholars had already said was true. By now he had "given up on salvation by faith alone," but he soon discovered that nowhere does the Bible teach *sola scriptura* either, so he tossed that out. (That Hahn could not even answer the question of a student—"Where does the Bible teach Scripture *alone* is authoritative and *not* church tradition?"—indicates that there was a very serious problem somewhere, and that it wasn't with Scripture.)

Hahn claims to have called the "top [evangelical] theologians in the country" and found that not *one* of them had an answer in defense of scriptural authority over tradition! (Somehow he never contacted the hundreds we know.) Nevertheless, despite tradition being errant and Scripture being inerrant, Hahn concluded that the doctrine of *sola scriptura* "wasn't scriptural."

All this had occurred by age 26. He claims he was then asked to become dean of the seminary he was teaching at. In good conscience he had to decline because he realized he was becoming a Catholic. He also stepped down from his pastorate and teaching job in a further attempt to resolve the issue. He next read some 200 books by Roman Catholic scholars. He also sought help from Catholics—for example, first from a priest who apparently did nothing but use swear words and was anything but a Christian; and second from a local Newman Center staff member, who apparently told him he could do more by staying within Protestantism and attempting to influence Protestants with Catholic ideas.

To illustrate the impact of his many studies in Catholicism, he makes statements such as the following: "I had worked literally through, I would guess, a hundred different doctrines that the

Catholic Church taught that the Protestant Church rejected, and I came out Catholic on every one of them." Given the fact that he had read some 200 books by Roman Catholic scholars, this may not be surprising.

Hahn now enrolled in a doctoral program in Roman Catholic systematic theology. This apparently cemented his commitment to Roman Catholicism, and he officially converted. Not unexpectedly, before long he fell "head over heels in love with the Virgin Mary," although this was the most difficult of Catholic doctrines for him to accept. Yet soon he was praying the Rosary to Mary every day—indeed he is now convinced that Mary supernaturally and regularly answers his prayers. He believes that prayer to Mary is one of the most powerful tools and weapons a Christian can have. "The real, supernatural proof of [the truth of Roman Catholicism] is Marian devotion." He tells the parish that the Rosary will "supernaturalize" a Catholic's faith.

At the end of his lecture he urges his audience to "*pray* about what you can do to be a witness to the glory and the truth of the Catholic faith."

What Scott Hahn's life illustrates is not the truth of Catholicism, but the perils of apostasy—one of the most serious matters one can encounter in life. Hahn's tapes and books have been much used by "evangelical" Catholics and other Roman Catholics in the attempt to convert evangelicals to their faith. Even his own wife, whom he describes as "the daughter of one of the most noted evangelical leaders in America," is "very, very close" to being converted to Catholicism. "On point after point, without a single exception, she has come to see how biblical the Roman Catholic faith is on everything."

The tragedy of Scott Hahn is not only with Scott Hahn; it is with the many other naïve evangelicals he has converted to Roman Catholicism. He and others like him no longer preach the gospel—they actively oppose it. And for this they are accountable.

Recommended Resources

For additional study we recommend the following:

Books:

Martin Luther, *Commentary on Galatians*, modern translation

James McCarthy, *The Gospel According to Rome* (Harvest House, 1995)

Ron Rhodes, *The Ten Most Important Things You Can Say to a Catholic* (Harvest House, 2002)

James White, *Justification by Faith* (Crown Publications, 1991)

Web Sites:

Alpha & Omega Ministries: www.aomin.org

Ankerberg Theological Research Institute: www.johnankerberg.org

Apologetics Index: www.apologeticsindex.org

Christian Resources: www.christiantruth.com

Notes

To the Reader: Full references are supplied only once. For convenience, a listing of main references follows these notes.

Understanding and Evaluating Roman Catholicism

1. Karl Keating, *What Catholics Really Believe—Setting the Record Straight* (Ann Arbor, MI: Servant, 1992), 112.

2. Robert C. Broderick, ed., *The Catholic Encyclopedia*, revised and updated (Nashville, TN: Thomas Nelson Publishers, 1987), 597. (Granted the *Nihil obstat* and *Imprimatur* of the Roman Catholic Church.)

3. Emmett McLoughlin, *Crime and Immorality in the Catholic Church* (New York: Lyle Stuart, 1964), 19.

1. How Influential Is the Roman Catholic Church in the World?

1. Adherents.com; www.cathnews.com/news/205/27.php (Accessed May 7, 2002).

2. What Are the Groupings Found in Roman Catholicism Today, and Why Are They Important for Understanding Catholicism?

1. H. J. Schroeder, tr., *The Canons and Decrees of the Council of Trent* (Rockford, IL: Tan Books, 1978), 150 (Canon 9 on the sacrifice of the Mass).

2. Lausanne Committee for World Evangelization, "Christian Witness to Nominal Christians Among Roman Catholics," *The Thailand Report on Roman Catholics* (Wheaton, IL: Lausanne Committee, 1980), 10.

3. Broderick, ed., 372.

4. H.M. Carson, *Dawn or Twilight? A Study of Contemporary Roman Catholicism* (Leicester, England: InterVarsity Press, 1976), 36; cf. Broderick, ed., *Catholic Encyclopedia*, 107, 469, 521-22; James Neher, *A Christian's Guide to Today's Catholic Charismatic Movement* (Hatfield, PA: James Neher, 1977).

3. Why Is a Book on Catholicism Relevant to Protestants and Vice Versa?

1. E.g., see James White, "Sola Scriptura in Dialogue," http://aomin.org/SS.html.

4. Is the Bible Alone the Final Authority, or Is It the Church?

1. Broderick, ed., 581.

2. John Paul II, *Ad Tuendam Fidem (In Order to Safeguard the Faith)*, May 28, 1998.

3. Karl Keating, *Catholicism and Fundamentalism: The Attack on "Romanism" by "Bible Christians"* (San Francisco: Ignatius Press, 1988), 275.

4. www.amazon.com/exec/obidos/tg/detail/-/1565071077/ref=cm_cr_dp_2_1/102-2766035-9674565?v=glance&s=books&vi=customer-reviews.

5. Why Do Protestants Believe that the Bible Alone Is Authoritative and Inerrant (Free from Error)?

1. Norman Geisler and William Nix, *A General Introduction to the Bible* (Chicago: Moody Press, 1971), 62, 66.

2. Ibid., 87; cf. Romans 3:2; 2 Timothy 3:15; 2 Peter 1:20-21.

3. Ibid., 88.

4. Ibid., 91, 97. Examples of New Testament claims for divine inspiration include Hebrews 1:1-2; 1 Corinthians 2:1,7,10,12-13; Galatians 1:11-12; Ephesians 5:26; 1 Thessalonians 2:13; 4:8; James 1:18; 1 Peter 1:25; 2 Peter 3:2, 16; 1 Timothy 4:1; Revelation 1:1-3; 22:18-19.

5. For a listing, see John Ankerberg and John Weldon, *Ready With an Answer* (Eugene, OR: Harvest House Publishers, 1997), 320-323.

6. As quoted by Harold Lindsell, *The Battle for the Bible* (Grand Rapids, MI: Zondervan, 1977), 67. For a fuller treatment see Ankerberg and Weldon, *Ready,* chs. 14-15.

6. How Do We Know that Claims for the Divine Inspiration and Inerrancy of the Bible Are Justified?

1. See e.g., J. Barton Payne, *The Encyclopedia of Biblical Prophecy* (Grand Rapids, MI: Baker, 1989), passim; John Ankerberg and John Weldon, *The Case for Jesus the Messiah* (Eugene, OR: Harvest House Publishers, 1989); Ankerberg and Weldon, *Ready,* appropriate chapters.

2. John Wenham, *Christ and the Bible* (Downers Grove, IL: InterVarsity, 1973), chs. 1-2,5; and the additional references in note 16 in John Ankerberg and John Weldon, *The Facts on Roman Catholicism* (Eugene, OR: Harvest House Publishers, 2003).

3. Ankerberg and Weldon, *Ready,* 308-311.

4. Ibid., relevant chs. and notes.

5. Gleason L. Archer, *Encyclopedia of Bible Difficulties* (Grand Rapids, MI: Zondervan, 1982), 11-12.

6. Robert Dick Wilson, *A Scientific Investigation of the Old Testament,* 13, 20, 130, 162-63; David Otis Fuller, ed., *Which Bible?* rev. ed. (Grand Rapids, MI: Grand Rapids International Publications, 1971), 44.

7. John Warwick Montgomery, *The Shape of the Past* (Bloomington, MN: Bethany House, 1975), 176.

8. Harold O.J. Brown, "The Arian Connection: Presuppositions of Errancy," in Gordon Lewis and Bruce Demarest, *Challeges to Inerrancy: A Theological Response* (Chicago: Moody, 1984), 389.

9. James I. Packer, *Beyond the Battle for the Bible* (Westchester, IL: Cornerstone Books, 1980), 43.

7. Why Are the Biblical Doctrines of Salvation and Justification So Remarkable?

1. "And the reason why they do not go down to hell at each moment, is not because God, in whose power they are, is not then very angry with them; as he is with many miserable creatures now tormented in hell, who there feel and bear the fierceness of his wrath. Yea, God is a great deal more angry with great numbers that are now on earth: yea, doubtless, with many that are now in this congregation, who it may be are at ease, than he is with many of those who are now in the flames of hell....All wicked men's pains and contrivance which they use to escape hell, while they continue to reject Christ, and so remain wicked men, do not secure them from hell one moment. Almost every natural man that hears of hell, flatters himself that he shall escape it; he depends upon himself for his own security; he flatters himself in what he has done, in what he is now doing, or what he intends to do....That

world of misery, that lake of burning brimstone, is extended abroad under you. There is the dreadful pit of the glowing flames of the wrath of God; there is hell's wide gaping mouth open; and you have nothing to stand upon, nor any thing to take hold of; there is nothing between you and hell but the air; it is only the power and mere pleasure of God that holds you up.

"You probably are not sensible of this; you find you are kept out of hell, but do not see the hand of God in it; but look at other things, as the good state of your bodily constitution, your care of your own life, and the means you use for your own preservation. But indeed these things are nothing; if God should withdraw his hand....The God that holds you over the pit of hell, much as one holds a spider, or some loathsome insect over the fire, abhors you, and is dreadfully provoked: his wrath towards you burns like fire; he looks upon you as worthy of nothing else, but to be cast into the fire; he is of purer eyes than to bear to have you in his sight; you are ten thousand times more abominable in his eyes, than the most hateful venomous serpent is in ours. You have offended him infinitely more than ever a stubborn rebel did his prince; and yet it is nothing but his hand that holds you from falling into the fire every moment....Now God stands ready to pity you; this is a day of mercy; you may cry now with some encouragement of obtaining mercy. But when once the day of mercy is past, your most lamentable and dolorous cries and shrieks will be in vain; you will be wholly lost and thrown away of God, as to any regard to your welfare....

"It would be dreadful to suffer this fierceness and wrath of Almighty God one moment; but you must suffer it to all eternity. There will be no end to this exquisite horrible misery. When you look forward, you shall see a long forever, a boundless duration before you, which will swallow up your thoughts, and amaze your soul; and you will absolutely despair of ever having any deliverance, any end, any mitigation, any rest at all. You will know certainly that you must wear out long ages, millions of millions of ages, in wrestling and conflicting with this almighty merciless vengeance; and then when you have so done, when so many ages have actually been spent by you in this manner, you will know that all is but a point to what remains. So that your punishment will indeed be infinite. Oh, who can express what the state of a soul in such circumstances is! All that we can possibly say about it, gives but a very feeble, faint representation of it; it is inexpressible and inconceivable: For 'who knows the power of God's anger?'...How dreadful is the state of those that are daily and hourly in the danger of this great wrath and infinite misery! But this is the dismal case of every soul in this congregation that has not been born again, however moral and strict, sober and religious, they may otherwise be. Oh that you would consider it, whether you be young or old! There is reason to think, that there are many in this congregation now hearing this discourse, that will actually be the subjects of this very misery to all eternity....[The] case [of those in hell] is past all hope; they are crying in extreme misery and perfect despair; but here you are in the land of the living and in the house of God, and have an opportunity to obtain salvation. What would not those poor damned hopeless souls give for one day's opportunity such as you now enjoy!" (http://www.ccel.org/e/edwards/sermons/sinners.html).

8. What Is the Biblical Proof for the Doctrine of Justification by Faith Alone?

1. As cited in Norman Geisler, prepublication manuscript on Roman Catholicism, 35.

2. Ibid., 34, citing Anthony A. Hoekema, *Saved by Grace* (Grand Rapids, MI: Eerdmans,1989), 154, and Millard J. Erickson, *Christian Theology* (Grand Rapids, MI: Baker, 1987), 955.

3. Hans Küng, *Justification* (Philadelphia: Westminster, 1964), 209; Geisler observes, "For an extended treatment of the Old Testament understandings of these terms and the difficulties inherent in translating from the Hebrew into Greek and Latin, see Alister E. McGrath,

Lustitia Dei, vol. 1, Cambridge University Press, 1986, pp. 4-16" (from Geisler, prepublication manuscript).

4. E.g., Geisler, prepublication manuscript, 29.

5. Broderick, ed., 319.

9. What Is the Dictionary Definition of *Justification?*

1. Gerhard Kittel, ed., *Theological Dictionary of the New Testament,* vol. 2 (Grand Rapids, MI: Eerdmans, 1978), 215-16.

2. Statements by Bruce Metzger as cited by Dr. Rod Rosenbladt in "The Salvation Debate" (with Karl Keating) conducted at the Simon Greenleaf School of Law, Anaheim, CA, March 11, 1989, cassette tape.

3. Copyright date and location within given sources, in order listed: 1984, p. 23; 1967, p. 196; 1977, p. 150; 1988, p. 557; 1966, p. 285.

11. What Does Roman Catholicism Teach About the Doctrines of Salvation and Justification?

1. *Catechism of the Catholic Church* (Liguori, MO: Liguori Publications, 1994), 1, 5-6 (emphasis added).

2. Ibid., 489-90.

3. As quoted in the *Los Angeles Times,* March 8, 1983, part I, 10.

4. Ludwig Ott, *Fundamentals of Catholic Dogma* (Rockford IL: Tan Books and Publishers, 1974), 264.

5. Peter Toon, *Foundations for Faith: Justification and Sanctification* (West Chester, IL: Crossway, 1983), 84; as cited in Geisler, prepublication manuscript.

6. H.J. Schroeder, tr., 36 (Canon 7).

7. Ibid. (Canon 9).

8. Ibid., 53 (Canon 7).

9. Ibid., 46 (Canon 32).

10. As cited in editorial "What Separates Evangelicals and Catholics," *Christianity Today,* October 23, 1981, 14-15, emphasis added.

12. Is Salvation Through Accepting Catholic Beliefs?

1. John Hardon, *The Question and Answer Catholic Catechism* (Garden City: Image, 1981); as cited in William Webster, "Saving Faith: How does Rome Define It? Is There a Basis for Unity Between Roman Catholicism and Evangelical Protestantism?" (http://www.christiantruth.com/savingfaithand rome.html).

13. Do Catholics and Protestants Mean the Same Things by the Words They Use?

1. John Warwick Montgomery, *The Shape of the Past* (Minneapolis: Bethany, 1975).

2. We demonstrated this thoroughly in John Ankerberg and John Weldon, *Protestants and Catholics: Do They Now Agree?* (Eugene, OR: Harvest House Publishers, 1995), chs. 10-11.

3. Anne Fremantle, *The Papal Encyclicals in Their Historical Context: The Teachings of the Popes* (New York: New American Library/Mentor, 1956), 11.

4. Keating, *Catholicism and Fundamentalism,* 81.

5. Fremantle, 11.

6. Keating, *What Catholics Really Believe,* 29.

7. Fremantle, 18.

14. Does the Bible Teach that, in *This* Life, There Is a True and Permanent Guarantee of Entering Heaven?

1. See our *Knowing the Truth about Eternal Security* (Eugene, OR: Harvest House Publishers, 1997).

15. What Are Some Personal Consequences of Catholic Theology?

1. Benny Diaz, "Why I Left The Roman Catholic Church (Part I)" (http://aomin.org/why_I_left.html).

2. Walter Martin, *The Roman Catholic Church in History* (Livingston, NJ: Christian Research Institute, 1960), 67.

3. Keating, *What Catholics Really Believe*, 66-67.

4. Keating, *Catholicism and Fundamentalism*, 166.

5. Ibid., 166-68, 175.

6. Joseph F. Bernard, "My Ticket to Heaven" (Patton, PA: n.d.), 3-10.

7. Cf. William J. Cogan, *A Catechism for Adults* (Youngtown, AZ: Cogan Productions, 1975), 50; as cited in James G. McCarthy, *Catholicism: Crisis of Faith*, video documentary annotated transcript (Lumen Productions, P.O. Box 595, Cupertino, CA 95015), 31.

16. What Are the Seven Sacraments?

1. John Paul II, *Crossing the Threshold of Faith* (New York: Alfred A. Knopf, 1994), 74-75.

2. Broderick, ed., 65.

3. Ibid., 131, 319.

4. Ibid., 466-68, 319; 105, 254; 466, (see Ott, 425); 467.

5. Ibid., 375-76.

6. Ibid., 372.

7. Ibid., 39-40, 208.

8. Ibid., 438-39.

9. Carson, 36; cf. Neher.

10. *Catechism* (1994), 289.

17. What Is the Alleged Power of the Sacraments?

1. http://www.newadvent.org/docs/pa06mf.htm.

2. *Catechism* (1994), 292.

3. Ott, 340-41.

4. *Catechism* (1994), 292.

5. Ibid., 246, 253.

6. Keating, in "The Salvation Debate."

7. McLoughlin, 17.

18. How Do Catholic and Protestant Views of the Sacraments Differ?

1. Schroeder, tr., 51 (7th session, March 3, 1547).

2. Ibid., 149-50.

3. Ibid., 52.

4. Ott, 264.

19. What Is the Mass?

1. Keating, *What Catholics Really Believe*, 53, emphasis added.

2. *Catechism* (1994), 334, 336.

3. Ibid., 346.

4. Ibid., 351.

5. Ibid., 347.

6. Council of Trent, Dz [Denzinger] 888; as cited in http://www.sspx.org/principles.html#p7.

7. *Catechism* (1994), 344.

8. Ibid., 345 (emphasis added).

9. Ibid., 351-52 (emphasis added).

10. See the fuller treatment in our *Catholics and Protestants,* 72-73, 76-78; and the sections in *Catechism* (1994) and Schroeder, tr.

11. Pope John Paul II, *Crossing the Threshold of Hope* (New York: Knopf, 1995), 139.

20. How Does the Mass Impact Christ's Atonement?

1. Carson, 111.

2. John Hardon, *The Catholic Catechism: The Contemporary Catechism of the Teachings of the Catholic Church* (Garden City, NY: Doubleday, 1975), 468.

3. Ott, 407, 412.

4. Schroeder, tr., 146 (7th Session, Canon 1).

5. *Mediator Dei,* part 2, chapter 1, 72; as cited in Carson, 112.

6. Ibid., 113.

7. Abbott, ed., 543.

8. Keating, *Catholicism and Fundamentalism,* 248.

9. Rev. John A. O'Brien, as quoted in ibid., 248.

10. Carson, 111.

11. Ibid., 112.

22. What Is Penance?

1. Broderick, ed., 254, 476, 466; cf. Ott, 425.

2. Broderick, ed., 467.

3. Schroeder, tr., 102 (14th Session, Canon 2); 39.

4. *Catechism* (1994), 363 (brackets in original).

5. Ibid., 361, 357.

6. Ibid., 366.

7. Broderick, ed., 402; cf. 466-68.

23. What Are Indulgences?

1. *Catechism* (1994), 370.

2. Keating, *What Catholics Really Believe,* 91.

3. Ott, 441.

4. Keating, *What Catholics Really Believe,* 95.

5. Broderick, ed., 291.

6. http://www.sev.org/members/tom.syperski/Journal2-5-03.html.

7. *Catechism* (1994), 370.

8. Ibid., 371.

9. *Outlines of Catholic Faith* (St. Paul, MN: Leaflet Missal Company, 1978), 43.

10. Keating, *What Catholics Really Believe,* 92.

11. Martin Luther, "Disputation on the Power and Efficacy of Indulgences Commonly Known as the 95 Theses," John Dillenberger, *Martin Luther: A Selection From His Writings* (New York: Doubleday, 1961); as cited in (http://aomin.org/95THESES.html).

12. Broderick, ed., 553.

13. Ibid., 529.

14. Ibid., 105.

15. Ibid., 291.

24. What Is the Rosary?

1. Cf. St. Louis De Montfort, *The Secret of the Rosary*, Mary Barbour, tr. (Bay Shore, NY: Montfort Publications, 1976), passim (this text contains the *Nihil obstat* and *Imprimatur*); cf. *Catechism* (1994), 253, 650.

2. Pope Paul VI, *Devotion to the Blessed Virgin Mary [Marialis Cultus]* (Washington, DC: United States Catholic Conference, 1974), 31.

3. http://www.vatican.va/holy_father/john_paul_ii/apost_letters/documents/hf_jpii_apl_200 21016 _rosarium-virginis-mariae_en.html.

4. Pope Paul VI, 37.

5. See "Rosary" in *The Catholic Encyclopedia,* vol. 13 (New York: The Encyclopedia Press, 1913), 184, 187.

6. Montfort, 47, 70, 86.

7. Ibid., 120, 123.

8. Ibid., 65.

25. What Is Purgatory?

1. "An In-Channel Debate on Purgatory" (http://aomin.org/ChanDeb1.html).

2. Keating, *What Catholics Really Believe,* 86.

3. The three views of purgatory are: a temporal (noneternal), literal hell; a temporal, literal hell with simultaneous experience of the bliss of Christ; a modified punishment less than hellish, but still severe.

4. Hardon, *The Catholic Catechism,* 273.

5. Broderick, ed., 117.

6. Ott, 485.

7. Schroeder, 274.

8. Ibid., 263-74.

9. Broderick, ed., 502.

26. Who Is Mary According to Rome?

1. David F. Wells, *Revolution in Rome* (Downer's Grove, IL: InterVarsity, 1972), 132.

2. Pope Paul VI, 20.

3. Abbott, ed., 94-95.

27. In Her Role as Co-Redemptrix, Does Mary Function as Another Savior?

1. Broderick, ed., 370.

2. In James White, "Many Thanks, Honorius" (http://aomin.org/ThanksHonor.html), emphasis added.

3. As cited in R.C. Sproul, "The Virgin Mary," manuscript, 5, emphasis added.

4. Ibid., 6; cf., Ott, 203-213, emphasis added.

5. Pope Paul VI, 15, emphasis added.

6. Abbott, ed., 91, 88, emphasis added.

7. Schrotenboer, ed., 37, 40, emphasis added.

8. Peter J. Stravinskas, *The Catholic Response* (Huntington IN: Our Sunday Visitor, 1985), 80, emphasis added.

9. Broderick, ed., 285, emphasis added.

10. Ott, 213, emphasis added.

11. Hardon, *The Catholic Catechism,*166-169, emphasis added.

28. Is Mary Worshiped in the Roman Catholic Church?

1. Catholicism teaches that the term *adoration,* "refers to the external act of worship or honor" (Broderick, ed, 24); "This cult of adoration [of the Host, who is Christ]…therefore, the Church commands that we adore Christ hidden under the Eucharistic veils" (ibid., 523; cf., 33).

2. Broderick, ed., 374, emphasis added.

3. Broderick, ed., 380.

4. Ibid., 32.

29. Who Is Mary According to the Bible?

1. Keating, *Catholicism and Fundamentalism,* 275; 279, emphasis added.

2. Ott, 200.

3. Keating, *Catholicism and Fundamentalism,* 282-89.

30. Are the Person and Work of Christ Compromised by Catholic Teachings?

1. Broderick, ed., 517, emphases added; 291, 502.

2. Ott, 213.

3. *Catechism* (1994), 166, emphasis added.

4. Keating, *Catholicism and Fundamentalism,* 44.

5. Broderick, ed., 24.

6. Tom Beaudoin, "The Cost of Economic Discipleship: U.S. Christians and Global Capitalism," Santa Clara Lecture, Santa Clara University, Nov. 4, 2001, n. 23 (http://www.scu.edu/bannancenter/SantaClaraLectures/BeaudoinLecture.htm).

7. Schrotenboer, ed., 21.

8. As cited in Gerrit C. Berkouwer, *The Conflict with Rome* (Philadelphia: Presbyterian & Reformed, 1958), 204-205.

9. Abbott, ed., 22.

10. Broderick, ed., 372.

32. What Is the Doctrine of Papal Infallibility?

1. Broderick, ed., 479. Recommended sources on the papacy: Richard McBrien, *Lives of the Popes;* Peter de Rosa, *Vicars of Christ;* Ludwig Pastor, *History of the Popes;* Halley, *Halley's Bible Handbook,* 767-793; John Foxe, *Foxe's Book of Martyrs,* ori. ed.; Eamon Duffy, *Saints and Sinners: A History of the Popes,* 2nd ed. J.N.D. Kelly, *Oxford Dictionary of Popes;* Paolo Prodi, tr., Susan Haskins, *The Papal Prince: One Body and Two Souls: The Papal Monarchy in Early Modern Europe;* and the Catholic yearbook, *Annuario Pontifico,* for specific years.

2. Ibid., 203, 292.

3. Ibid., 292.

4. Henry T. Hudson, *Papal Power* (Welwyn, Hertfordshire, England: Evangelical Press, 1981), 112.

5. Keating, *Catholicism and Fundamentalism*, 219; emphasis added.

6. Broderick, ed., 292, 596.

7. Ibid., 434.

8. As cited in Carson, 41-42.

9. R.C. Sproul, lecture on infallibility, undated photocopy on file.

10. *De Ecclesia*, 22, in Schrotenboer, ed., 51; cf., Broderick, ed., 296.

11. Keating, *What Catholics Really Believe*, p. 15; *De Ecclesia*, 25, in Schroetenboer, ed., 52; Keating, op. cit. 15; see also Broderick, ed., 292.

12. Broderick, ed., 188.

13. August Bernard Hasler, *How the Pope Became Infallible: Pius IX and the Politics of Persuasion* (Garden City, NY: Doubleday, 1981), 310.

14. Issued by the Holy Office (Acta Sanctae Sedis, X [1877], 71 ff.). Henricus Denzinger, Ed Schomelzer, eds., *Enchiridion Symbolorum* [Sources of Catholic Dogma], n. 994-1000 (Crossroad/Herder & Herder, 1998); as cited in http://www.catholiccontroversy.home-stead.com/Trent.html. See also Jesuit Fathers of St. Mary's College, St. Mary's, Kansas, *The Church Teaches* (Rockford, IL: Tan Books and Publishers, 1973), 8-9.

33. Is the Doctrine of Papal Infallibility Credible in Light of the Teachings and Decrees of Catholic Popes, and What Are the Consequences of This Doctrine?

1. Keating, *Catholicism and Fundamentalism*, 223.

2. Küng, *Infallible?: An Inquiry* (Garden City, NY: Image Books, 1972), 30.

3. Harold O.J. Brown, *Heresies: The Image of Christ in the Mirror of Heresy and Orthodoxy from the Apostles to the Present* (Garden City, NY: Doubleday, 1990), 66,186,190,207; Küng, *Infallible?*, 30; Carson, 83, 84-85.

4. Hudson, 112; Martin, 17-21.

5. Leonard Swidler, ed., *Küng in Conflict* (Garden City, NY: Doubleday, 1981), 33.

6. Hudson, 112; cf., the letter from Pope Pius VI to the Archbishop of Florence dated April 1778 on the title page of the Roman Catholic English Bible; cf., the Council of Toulon, 1239; the Council of Trent's Index of Prohibited Books, 4th rule; the encyclical letter of Pope Leo XII May 3, 1824, etc., as cited in Dreyer and Weller, *Roman Catholicism in the Light of Scripture* (Chicago: Moody Press, 1960), 13-16. References for papal infallibility include Carson, 80-85; cf., Broderick, ed., 479-82 for a list; cf., Richard Knolls, *Roman Catholicism: Issues and Evidences;* Martin, 17-20.

34. How Do Catholics and Protestants Differ as to the Books (Canon) of the Bible?

1. Other apocryphal books in the Septuagint—the Prayer of Manasseh and 1 and 2 Esdras are not declared to be inspired. Cf., Broderick, ed., *The Catholic Encyclopedia*, 160; *The Encyclopedia Britannica Micropaedia*, q.v. "Apocrypha," vol. 1, 446.

2. Schroeder, 18.

3. Keating, *What Catholics Really Believe*, 46; or Keating, *Catholicism and Fundamentalism*, 46.

35. Can One Know with Assurance that the Apocrypha Is Not Scripture?

1. See 2 Maccabees, Ecclesiasticus, Wisdom of Solomon, Tobit. Good general discussions on the Apocrypha include Bernard Ramm, *Protestant Christian Evidences* (Chicago: Moody Press, 1953); his article "The Apocrypha," (King's Business, July 1947, 15-17); David G. Dunbar, "The Biblical Canon," in D.A. Carson and John D. Woodbridge, eds., *Hermeneutics, Authority and Canon* (Grand Rapids, MI: Zondervan Academic Books, 1986); Allan MacRae, "The Canon of Scripture: Can We Be Sure Which Books Are Inspired by God?" in John Warwick Montgomery, ed., *Evidence for Faith: Deciding the God Question* (Dallas:

Probe, 1991). A helpful list of OT and NT apocryphal and pseudepigraphic writings can be found at, appropriately: www.pseudepigrapha.com, a lay LDS (Mormon) Web site.

2. *Zondervan Pictorial Encyclopedia of the Bible,* vol. 1, 207-210; cf., *Encyclopedia Britannica Macropaedia,* vol. II, 932ff.

3. René Pache, *The Inspiration and Authority of Scripture,* tr. Helen I. Needham (Chicago: Moody Press, 1969), 172.

4. R. Laird Harris, *Inspiration and Canonicity of the Bible,* 102.

5. Pache, 173; cf. James White, "The Early Canon Process of the New Testament" (http://aomin.org/earlycanon.html).

6. William Webster, "Did I Really Leave the Holy Catholic Church?" in John Armstrong, ed., *Roman Catholicism: Evangelical Protestants Analyze What Divides and Unites Us* (Chicago: Moody Press, 1994), 276.

7. Norman L. Geisler, Ralph MacKenzie, *Roman Catholics and Evangelicals: Agreements and Differences* (Grand Rapids, MI: Baker, 1995), 169.

8. R. Laird Harris, *Inspiration,* 184.

9. William Webster, "Did I Really Leave the Holy Catholic Church?" 277.

36. "Evangelicals and Catholics Together" I and II—What's the Bottom Line?

1. http://acts413.org/religions/catholic/ect_2doc.htm. For John Ankerberg's response to all three documents, see his Response Letter, available from the Ankerberg Theological Research Institute.

2. William Webster, "Why the Accords are Unacceptable and Are a Fundamental Denial of the Truth of the Gospel" (http://www.christiantruth.com/ECT.html).

3. From Webster, "Why the Accords are Unacceptable." A full documentation of these teachings can be found at ibid., "Saving Faith and Rome."

37. Why Do Some Protestants Join Rome?

1. Robert Baram, ed., *Spiritual Journeys: Toward the Fullness of Faith,* (Boston: Daughters of St. Paul, 1988), 154-155, 163, 167, and ff.

2. Ibid., 176, emphasis added.

3. Ibid., 177-178.

4. Ibid., 167.

5. Nancy M. Cross, "The Attraction of Evangelical Christians to Catholicism," *Homiletic and Pastoral Review,* December 1991, 53.

38. What Makes a Religion Christian?

1. Verbatim. Copy on file.

2. John Ankerberg and John Weldon, *Everything You Ever Wanted to Know About Mormonism* (Eugene, OR: Harvest House Publishers, 1992).

3. Broderick, ed., 371.

4. F.F. Bruce, *The Canon of Scripture* (Downers Grove, IL: InterVarsity Press, 1988), 262.

A Personal Word to Catholics—and Many Protestants

1. Broderick, ed., 270,402,585.

2. Ibid., 539.

Appendix A: Further Discussion of the "Evangelicals and Catholics Together" Declarations

1. R.C. Sproul, "What ECT Ignores: The Inseparable Link Between Imputation and the Gospel," *Modern Reformation* magazine, September/October 1998, vol. 7. Article found in Alliance of Confessing Evangelicals Web site (http://www.Christianity.com/partner/article_display_page 10, PTID307086/CHID559376/CIID1413798,00.html). By Permission of the Alliance of Confessing Evangelicals, 1716 Spruce St., Philadelphia, PA 19103, www.ModernReformation.org. Excerpted by permission of the author.

Appendix B: What Reasons Do Evangelicals Give for Converting to Roman Catholicism?

1. Baram, ed., *Spiritual Journeys,* 159.

2. Ibid., 160-162.

3. Ibid.

4. Ibid., 383-384, 387.

5. Ibid., 389.

6. Ibid., 391-392; 393.

7. Ibid., 167-169.

8. Ibid., 167,170.

9. Ibid., 173.

10. Tape on file.

BIBLIOGRAPHY OF
MAIN REFERENCES

Broderick, Robert C., ed. *The Catholic Encyclopedia,* rev. and updated. Nashville, TN: Thomas Nelson Publishers, 1987. (Granted the *Nihil obstat* and *Imprimatur* of the Roman Catholic Church.)

Catechism of the Catholic Church. Liguori, MO: Liguori Publications, 1994.

Keating, Karl. *Catholicism and Fundamentalism: The Attack on "Romanism" by "Bible Christians."* San Francisco: Ignatius Press, 1988.

————. *What Catholics Really Believe—Setting the Record Straight.* Ann Arbor, MI: Servant, 1992.

Ott, Ludwig. *Fundamentals of Catholic Dogma.* Rockford, IL: Tan Books and Publishers, 1974.

Schroeder, H.J., tr. *The Canons and Decrees of the Council of Trent.* Rockford, IL: Tan Books, 1978.